Also by Lauren Smith

Your Colors at Home
Colors for Brides
What Goes With What: Home Decorating Made Easy

This is the third book in Capital's What Goes With What series—a series that delves into various lifestyle topics and shows readers how to combine the vital elements of each to make a finished design in tune with their personal style. Other titles include:

What Goes With What: Home Decorating Made Easy, by Lauren Smith
   with Noemi C. Taylor
What Goes With What for Parties: Planning Made Easy by Bo Niles

What Goes With What: Dishes & Dining Rooms
Decorating Made Easy

LAUREN SMITH

CAPITAL BOOKS, INC.
Sterling, Virginia

Copyright © 2004 by Lauren Smith

All rights reserved. No part of this book may be reproduced or utilized in any form or by any means, electronic or mechanical, including photocopying, recording, or by any information storage and retrieval system, without permission in writing from the publisher. Inquiries should be addressed to:

Capital Books, Inc.
P.O. Box 605
Herndon, Virginia 20172-0605

ISBN 1-931868-28-X (alk. paper)

Library of Congress Cataloging-in-Publication Data

Smith, Lauren.
    What goes with what : dishes & dining rooms : decorating made easy / Lauren Smith.—1st ed.
       p. cm.
    Includes index.
    ISBN 1-931868-28-X (alk. paper)
      1. Table setting and decoration.   I. Title.
    TX871.S596   2004
    642'.6—dc22
                          2004006887

Printed in the United States of America on acid-free paper that meets the American National Standards Institute Z39-48 Standard.

First Edition

10 9 8 7 6 5 4 3 2 1

*To Robert Zone Smith, my late husband,
who indulged my passion for collecting china.*

CONTENTS

Introduction:	Why Dining Areas Are So Special	ix
Chapter 1.	Finding Your Style Style Quiz	1
Chapter 2.	Putting It All Together Determining Your Priorities Estimating Your Costs Setting the Timetable	7
Chapter 3.	Choosing Your Dining Room Furniture Periods and Styles Style Spanners What Goes With What Shopping for Furniture	13
Chapter 4.	Starting with Your China Selecting China Shopping for China Caring for Dinnerware Storing Dinnerware	35
Chapter 5.	Deciding on Your Silver Selecting Silver Shopping for Silver Hollowware Monograms Caring for Flatware Storing Flatware	47
Chapter 6.	Adding Your Crystal Selecting Crystal Shopping for Crystal Caring for Crystal Storing Crystal	59

Chapter 7.	Finishing with Your Table Linens	*69*
	Selecting Table Linens	
	Shopping for Table Linens	
	Monograms	
	Caring for Table Linens	
	Storing Table Linens	
Chapter 8.	Dressing Your Table	*77*
	Napkin Folds	
	Formal Dinner	
	Semi-formal Dinner	
	Luncheon	
	Dinner Buffet	
	Tea or Dessert Buffet	
Chapter 9.	Setting Your Table	*81*
	Formal Dinner	
	Semi-formal Dinner	
	Luncheon	
	Dinner Buffet	
	Tea or Dessert Buffet	
Chapter 10.	Decorating Your Table	*87*
	Fresh Flowers	
	Potted Plants	
	Accessories	
	Candles	
	Creative Decorations	
	Family Occasions	
	Holidays	

Resource Guide	*95*
Your Style at a Glance	*123*
Your Style at a Glance Worksheet	*126*
Index	*129*
Notes	*133*

Introduction

WHY DINING AREAS ARE SO SPECIAL

In this age of rush, rush, rush, the special time you spend with friends and family is often over a meal. Whether you have a small dining alcove or a separate dining room, whether you love to cook elaborate meals or order takeout, this place where you sit down with your family, entertain your friends, or simply relax by yourself, is an important place in your home.

Your dining area should be inviting and comfortable, and it should reflect your personal style—from your table and chairs to your tableware. To help you get started, take the Style Quiz in the next chapter. Determine whether you are a "true to tradition" or sophisticated urban formal-type person; a rather romantic semi-formal-type who appreciates the styles of the past but is more concerned with the comfort of your guests; or a fun-loving informal person who likes an element of surprise.

Once you determine your personal style, this book will show you not only how to find the right furnishings and tableware, but also how to put them all together in a room that fits your lifestyle. Through easy-to-use lists, charts, simple black-and-white drawings, and wise words, you will learn how to combine furnishings with tableware for the way you live—from daily dining to entertaining. Quickly and easily, discover how to dress, set, and accessorize your table for a luncheon, a dinner, a special occasion, or for simple everyday dining.

Whether you are on a tight budget or have more money to spend, at the end of the book you'll find a comprehensive list of resources for furniture, tableware, linens, and other decorating resources. I hope this book will be your answer to decorating a new dining room or redoing an old one—with simplicity and ease.

Chapter 1

FINDING YOUR STYLE

Dressing a dining room is a lot like dressing for a party. A formal occasion calls for silks, satins, jewels, and furs; an informal get-together, casual clothing; and a semi-formal occasion, something in between. Like parties, most furniture and tableware styles fall into three major categories: formal, semi-formal, and informal.

Style Quiz

The best way to determine your decorating style is to take the following style quiz. If none of the answers is exactly you, choose the one that is closest.

1. If you could live anywhere, it would be in a
   a. large city
   b. quiet suburb
   c. country village

2. An invitation you would like to receive would be for a
   a. dinner dance
   b. book signing
   c. wine tasting

3. The car you would most like to own is a
   a. Bentley
   b. Volvo
   c. Jeep

4. On your next vacation you would like to visit
   a. New York City
   b. Williamsburg
   c. Yellowstone Park

5. On an evening out, you would be likely to attend
   a. the opera or ballet
   b. a local playhouse
   c. an outdoor concert

6. You would most likely take a cooking course in
   a. classical French cooking
   b. new American cooking
   c. ethnic cooking

7. The style magazine you would likely subscribe to is
   a. *Vanity Fair*
   b. *House & Garden*
   c. *Real Simple*

8. Your favorite pet is a
   a. Lhasa apso
   b. springer spaniel
   c. calico cat

9. On a free Saturday, you would be likely to
   a. preview a furniture auction
   b. browse in a bookstore
   c. attend a street fair

10. After cleaning out your attic, you decide to
    a. refinish an antique chair
    b. restore old photographs
    c. turn it into a loft

11. On a beautiful spring day, you would likely
    a. go on a designer house tour
    b. work in your garden
    c. explore the countryside

12. On a rainy spring day, you would likely
    a. see a foreign film
    b. read a favorite book
    c. bake bread

13. If you had some spare time, you would volunteer at
    a. an art museum
    b. the public library
    c. an animal shelter

14. At an auction you would most likely bid on
    a. Chippendale chairs
    b. botanical prints
    c. hand-made quilts

15. In your dining room, you would like to have a
    a. Georgian-style fireplace
    b. large window with a garden view
    c. high ceiling with open beams

16. When you entertain at home, you usually have a
    a. sit-down dinner
    b. buffet dinner
    c. brunch or lunch

17. The wood you would like for your table is
    a. polished mahogany
    b. mellow fruitwood
    c. scrubbed pine

18. For your chandelier, you would choose
    a. crystal
    b. brass or pewter
    c. wood or iron

19. Under your table, you would like to have a
    a. hand-made Oriental rug
    b. needlepoint rug
    c. sisal rug

20. For your windows, you might choose
    a. Austrian shades
    b. valance and side panels
    c. tab curtains

Now add how many *a*'s, *b*'s, and *c*'s you have chosen, and look below to find your personal decorating style.

FORMAL

If you answered mostly *a*'s, your decorating style is formal. Whatever style you choose, you are true to tradition and try to duplicate the look as authentically as possible. You would like fine antiques but you also know the value of good reproductions. Your dream is to have a dining room with a mahogany double-pedestal table and carved chairs, a crystal chandelier, and an Oriental rug.

SEMI-FORMAL

If you answered mostly *b*'s, your decorating style is semi-formal. While you appreciate the styles of the past, you are more concerned with comfort than authenticity. You decorate with a personal touch, combining adaptations with family collectibles. Your dream dining room is likely to have a mellow wood table and chairs with soft upholstered backs and dressmaker skirts, a brass chandelier, and a needlepoint rug.

INFORMAL

If you answered mostly *c*'s, your decorating style is informal. Whether you use antiques or reproductions, you are more interested in fun than formality. You like an element of surprise and whatever you do is insouciant and charming. Your dream of a dining room is to pair a scrubbed pine table with painted chairs, a wrought-iron chandelier, and a sisal rug.

ECLECTIC

You might find that your answers fall almost equally into two or even three categories. If so, your decorating style is eclectic and combines the best from different periods. Chapter 3 on choosing furniture will give you some guidelines.

PUTTING IT ALL TOGETHER

Now that you know your personal style, you may be wondering how to get started and how to fit all your plans into your budget.

First of all, you do *not* have to do it all at one time. You may do one thing at a time if you have a plan in mind. To make your plan, you will have to make some decorating decisions in order to determine your priorities, estimate your costs, and set up a time schedule.

Determining Your Priorities

To help you determine your priorities, use the chart at the end of this chapter to begin planning your dining area. List the dining room furnishings; wall, floor, and window coverings; and the table appointments you *have,* what you *need*, and what you *want*. For example, if your walls are in bad condition, you *need* to paint; but you may *want* to add a chair rail, crown molding, or wainscoting. On the other hand, if you have just moved into a new home and have a completely empty dining room with no architectural features at all, you may *need* to add these style-defining details *before* painting or purchasing furnishings, so put these expenses into your "need" column instead of the more distant "want" column. Once you have separated your *needs* from your *wants*, you will be able to determine your priorities.

Estimating Your Costs

In later chapters you'll find information on choosing furnishings and table appointments. Read ahead if you would like, then come back to fill in your chart with the choices you need and what you want to purchase in the future. You will also have to estimate the cost of the furnishings, lighting, floorcovering, wallcovering, and window treatments you want.

Lighting includes *hanging fixtures* such as *chandeliers* and *pendants*, *recessed lighting*, and *track lighting*.

To estimate the cost of a hanging fixture, you will have to know what size fixture you need. In order to estimate the right size, take the average size of your walls and multiply by two. For example, if your dining room is 13 feet $\times$ 15 feet, your average wall is 14 feet, so your fixture should be about 28 inches in diameter.

If you are considering recessed or track lighting, you will have to call in a professional to assess your needs and give you an estimate.

Floor coverings include *carpet* and *rugs*. To estimate the amount of carpet you will need for wall-to-wall installation, multiply the width and length of your room to get the square feet. Then divide the number of square feet by nine to get the number of square yards. For example, if your room is 13 $\times$ 15, or 195 square feet, you will need 21.66 or about 22 square yards.

An *area rug* used underneath a dining table should be at least four feet longer and wider than the table. A *room-size rug* should have a margin of twelve to eighteen inches of hard flooring all around. If your floors are in bad condition, you will also have to estimate the cost of refinishing or even replacing your floors.

Wall coverings include *paint* and *wallpaper*. To estimate the amount of *paint* you will need, add up the length and width of all the walls in the room. If you have a standard eight-foot ceiling, multiply that number by eight to get the square feet. For every 250 to 350 square feet, you will need about one gallon of paint—depending on the condition of the walls.

You will also have to estimate paint or stain for the trim, and if the ceiling needs to be painted, you will also have to include that in your estimate. Always buy a little more than you need for touch-ups.

To estimate the amount of *wallpaper* you will need, measure all the walls including windows and doors. If you have a standard eight-foot ceiling, multiply by eight and divide by thirty. Then subtract one-half roll for each standard-size window and door. For example, if your dining room is 13 × 15, you will need fifteen rolls less one-half roll for every window and door. Add 10 percent for every ten inches of pattern repeat. Again, buy a little more than you actually need.

Before you decide whether to paint or paper or both, you will have to decide whether existing architectural details are in keeping with the style of the room and, if your room does not have any details at all, whether to add them. Crown molding, chair rails, and wainscoting are readily available in a wide variety of period styles. Keep in mind, a chair rail should be installed one-third of the way up the wall and will serve as a divider between your wainscoting and contrasting paint or paper, so you will have to estimate your paint and paper accordingly. If you are not going to do everything yourself, you will also have to estimate the cost of labor.

Window treatments include *hard treatments* such as *blinds*, *shutters*, and *screens*, and *soft treatments* such as *curtains* with or without top treatments, and *fabric shades*.

To estimate the cost of your window treatments, measure the width and length of the window including the frame, and the width and length of the window inside the frame. Then measure the width and length of the whole wall. On a sheet of paper, draw the wall including the window, and note your measurements on your drawing, including the length from the top of the frame to the ceiling and from the bottom of the frame to the floor and also the width on each side of the window frame to the wall. Take your drawing and a picture of your dining room furniture and carpet, fabric, and wallpaper samples with you. The store decorator will help you decide what type of window treatment or combination of treatments is right for your windows and your room, and give you an estimate.

Setting the Timetable

Add up all your estimates, including your needs and wants in all categories. Then set up a timetable according to your budget. For example, if your needs and wants total $18,000 and you are able to spend $7,500 a year, it will take you about 2½ years; but if you are only able to spend $5,000 a year, it will take you about 3½ years. If you need to finish your project right away, consider using a deferred payment plan or taking out a home equity loan.

MY DINING AREA PLANNING CHART				
Type	What I Have	What I Need	What I Want	Estimated Cost
Furnishings				
Table				
Armchairs				
Side chairs				
Other				
Lighting				
Chandelier				
Pendants				
Recessed lighting				
Track lighting				
Floor coverings				
Flooring				
Carpet				
Rug				
Wall coverings				
Paint				
Wallpaper				
Millwork				
Chair rail				
Crown molding				
Wainscoting				
Window treatments				
Blinds				
Shades				
Shutters				
Screens				
Curtains				
China				
Place settings				
Dinner plates				
Salad plates				
Bread and butter plates				
Cups				

My Dining Area Planning Chart *(continued)*

Type	What I Have	What I Need	What I Want	Estimated Cost
Saucers				
Soup plates				
Dessert plates				
Creamer and sugar bowl				
Coffee pot				
Teapot				
Platters				
Vegetable dishes				
Silver				
Place settings				
Teaspoons				
Knives				
Forks				
Salad forks				
Cream soup spoons				
Butter spreaders				
Place spoons				
Meat fork				
Carving set				
Two-piece steak set				
Sugar spoon				
Gravy ladle				
Butter and cake knives				
Crystal				
Goblets				
Red wine glasses				
White wine glasses				
Champagne glasses				
Cordial glasses				
Table Linens				
Tablecloths				
Napkins				
Placemats				
Runners				

Chapter 3

CHOOSING YOUR DINING ROOM FURNITURE

Dining room furniture should set the style for or support the style of your tableware. The table is the focal point of the room. It should define the size and shape of the room, establish a historic period, and set the mood of the room: *formal, semi-formal*, or *informal*.

FORMAL

- Queen Anne
- Georgian, including Chippendale, Hepplewhite, and Sheraton
- Regency
- Federal, including Hepplewhite, Sheraton, and Duncan Phyfe
- Louis XV
- Louis XVI
- Gustavian
- Victorian
- Contemporary

SEMI-FORMAL

- Early English
- Colonial American, including Queen Anne and Chippendale
- French Provincial

- Italian Provincial
- Swedish Provincial
- American Victorian

INFORMAL

- Country English
- Early American
- Country French
- Country Italian
- Country Swedish
- Cottage Victorian
- Farmhouse Victorian
- Southwest, including Adobe, Mission, and Santa Fe
- American Country, including Shaker and Pennsylvania Dutch
- Modern, including Bauhaus, High tech, Japanese, and Scandinavian
- Tropical
- Beach

Periods and Styles

Some words you will come across in furniture descriptions are *period*, *style*, and even *period style*. The word "style" refers to the use of certain design characteristics, while the word "period" refers to the duration of time when these characteristics were popularized. In some cases, such as the Queen Anne period, style and period coincide. In other cases, such as the Georgian period, it includes several styles.

In choosing a style that is appropriate to your room, the shape of the room and architectural details are a good guideline. For example, a well-proportioned room with classic architectural details and symmetrical windows suggests the Georgian style, while a room with an irregular shape and a bay window suggests Victorian style.

Once you have chosen a style, it is important not to be confined by it, but to use it as inspiration only. For example, combine a traditional Sheraton double-pedestal table with Queen Anne, Chippendale, Hepplewhite, or Duncan Phyfe chairs; or a contemporary glass table with Louis XV or Louis XVI chairs; or a modern Parsons table with Early American, Country English, or Country French chairs.

The woods you use do not have to match, but they should have the same feeling. For example, a maple table is not compatible with mahogany chairs, but a medium maple or scrubbed pine table mixes well with painted chairs.

Style Spanners

There are certain tables and chairs that span more than one style:

- Glass dining room tables with specific bases
- Parsons tables, painted, papered, or upholstered with specific patterns
- Parsons dining room chairs with skirts and specific fabrics

What Goes With What

In every period, there are certain features that characterize the style. Chair shapes and legs are the easiest to identify. The suggested patterns and colors listed below will help you to set the background for a style and *get the look*.

Formal

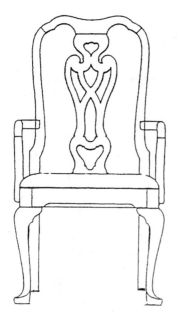

QUEEN ANNE

How to Get the Look

Patterns—formal textures such as moirés and striés

Colors—soft reds, yellows, blues, greens, grays, and whites

CHIPPENDALE

How to Get the Look

Patterns—formal textures such as damasks, brocades, and formal stripes

Colors—rich reds, yellows, blues, and greens; beiges, grays, and whites

HEPPLEWHITE

How to Get the Look

Patterns—formal textures such as damasks and narrow stripes

Colors—soft reds, yellows, blues, greens, beiges, grays, and whites, with a predominance of blues and greens

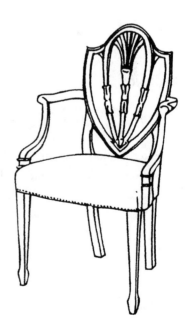

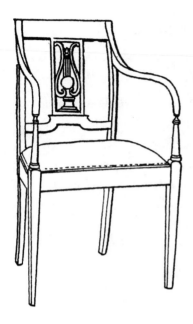

SHERATON

How to Get the Look

Patterns—formal textures such as brocades and formal stripes
Colors—soft reds, yellows, blues, greens, grays, and whites, with a predominance of blues

REGENCY

How to Get the Look

Patterns—formal textures such as brocades, damasks, and bold stripes
Colors—deep reds, yellows, blues, black, and whites

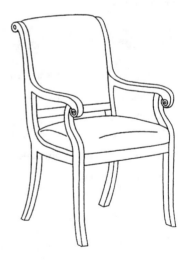

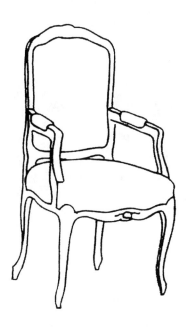

LOUIS XV

How to Get the Look

Patterns—formal textures and formal stripes
Colors—soft reds, yellows, blues, and greens; grays, beiges, and whites

LOUIS XVI

How to Get the Look

Patterns—formal textures and formal stripes
Colors—light reds, yellows, blues, and greens; beiges, grays, and whites

GUSTAVIAN

How to Get the Look

Patterns—formal textures and formal stripes
Colors—light cool blues, grays, and whites

FEDERAL

How to Get the Look

Patterns—formal textures and formal stripes
Colors—soft reds, yellows, blues, and greens; beiges, grays, and whites

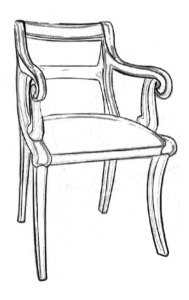

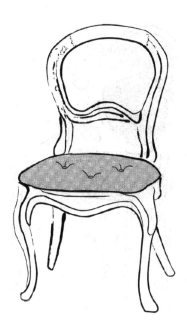

VICTORIAN

How to Get the Look

Patterns—formal textures including brocades and flocks
Colors—deep reds, greens, and whites

CONTEMPORARY

How to Get the Look

Patterns—formal textures and formal stripes
Colors—beiges, taupes, grays, browns, black, and whites

Semi-formal

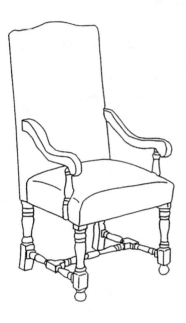

EARLY ENGLISH

> #### How to Get the Look
>
> Patterns—Jacobean florals, tree-of-life motifs, fruits, wreaths, oak leaves, and flamestitch
>
> Colors—earthy reds, yellows, blues, and greens; beiges, browns, black, and whites

COLONIAL AMERICAN

> #### How to Get the Look
>
> Patterns—reproduction prints including florals, fruits, and birds, architectural murals and chinoiserie
>
> Colors—medium to dark reds, yellows, blues, and greens; beiges, grays, and whites

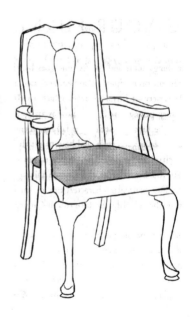

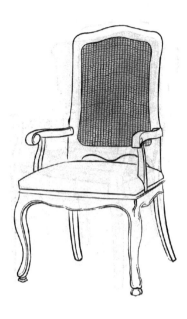

FRENCH PROVINCIAL

How to Get the Look

Patterns—toiles with floral and pastoral scenes, and ticking stripes
Colors—medium reds, yellows, blues, and greens; beiges, grays, and whites

ITALIAN PROVINCIAL

How to Get the Look

Patterns—toiles with classic Grecian and Roman scenes, and ticking stripes
Colors—medium reds, yellows, blues, and greens; beiges, grays, black, and whites.

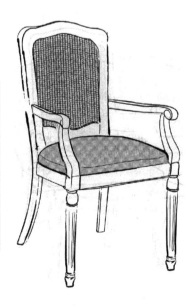

SWEDISH PROVINCIAL

How to Get the Look

Patterns—toiles and ticking stripes

Colors—medium reds, yellows, blues, grays, and whites, with a predominance of blue

AMERICAN VICTORIAN

How to Get the Look

Patterns—florals and floral stripes, cabbage roses in particular, and plain stripes

Colors—medium reds, yellows, blues, greens, and whites

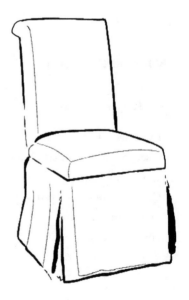

Informal

COUNTRY ENGLISH

How to Get the Look

Patterns—small paisley florals, all-over paisleys and paisley stripes

Colors—earthy reds, yellows, blues, and greens; beiges, browns, black, and whites

EARLY AMERICAN

How to Get the Look

Patterns—small florals, plaids, checks, stripes, and thematics such as Americana, nautical, and wildlife

Colors—earthy reds, yellow, and greens, with a predominance of blues, beiges, and browns

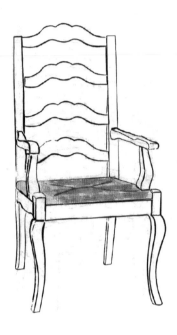

COUNTRY FRENCH

How to Get the Look

Patterns—small block-printed florals and fruits, checks, plaids, and stripes

Colors—bright reds, yellows, blues, and whites with a predominance of yellows and blues

COUNTRY ITALIAN

How to Get the Look

Patterns—small florals and fruits such as grapes, checks, plaids, and stripes

Colors—warm earthy reds, yellows, blues, greens, and whites

COUNTRY SWEDISH

How to Get the Look

Patterns—small floral sprigs, checks, plaids, and stripes
Colors—bright reds, yellows, blues, grays, and whites

COTTAGE VICTORIAN

How to Get the Look

Patterns—small florals, especially roses; plaids, checks, and stripes
Colors—light to bright reds, yellows, blues, greens, and whites

FARMHOUSE VICTORIAN

How to Get the Look

Patterns—small florals and floral stripes, plaids, checks, and stripes

Colors—medium to dark reds, yellows, blues, greens, and whites

SOUTHWEST

How to Get the Look

Patterns—geometrics such as American Indian blanket designs
Colors—brilliant vegetable-dye colors for Adobe and Mission; neutrals such as beiges, grays, whites, sunset browns, and dusty desert pastels for Santa Fe

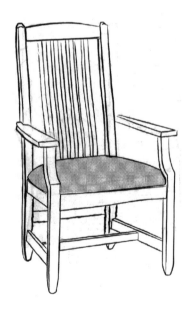

AMERICAN COUNTRY

How to Get the Look

Patterns—stencil designs, checks, plaids, and stripes
Colors—whites and beiges with accents of reds, yellows, blues, and greens

MODERN

How to Get the Look

Patterns—geometrics and stripes
Colors—whites, beiges, taupes, grays, browns, and black

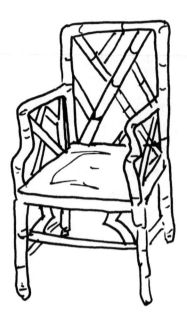

TROPICAL

How to Get the Look

Patterns—tropical florals, banana leaves, ferns, palm trees, animal prints, bamboo lattice, stripes, and thematics

Colors—light to bright to dark reds, yellows, blues, and greens; beiges, browns, black, and whites

BEACH

How to Get the Look

Patterns—seashells, sea oats, starfish, stripes, and nautical themes

Colors—light to medium greens and blues of the sea and sky, dark blues, dusty beach neutrals

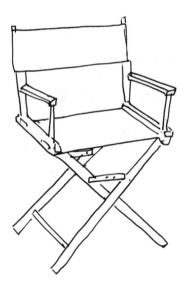

Shopping for Furniture

Furniture is sold in *suites*, *groups*, and *collections*.

A *suite* consists of basic pieces designed to be used together in one room and priced as a unit. For example, a dining room suite usually includes a table, chairs, and either a china cabinet, buffet, or sideboard.

A *group* consists of many pieces of furniture in the same style for every room, including the basic suite and many additional pieces. The advantage is that you can add pieces as your budget and space increase; the disadvantage is that you might wind up with a monotonous room if you are not clever with accessories.

A *collection* is usually more expensive. It consists of pieces that are not exactly the same style but have a feeling of compatibility. Your finished room will look as if it were made up of individual pieces collected over a period of time.

Before you buy any piece of furniture, read the tag for information. A tag may have a historical reference or indicate that the piece is an *antique*, *reproduction*, or *adaptation*. An *antique* is a piece of furniture that, according to U. S. law, must be at least one hundred years old. A *reproduction* is a line-for-line copy of the original piece, whereas an *adaptation* has some elements that have been adapted to fit present-day needs. A good *reproduction* will cost more than an *adaptation*, but you may be buying an antique of the future.

A tag will also tell you what type of wood was used and whether it is *solid*, *genuine*, or *veneer*. If a tag indicates it is made from *solid* wood, it means it is made from a solid hardwood; *genuine* means it is made from a single hardwood with veneer on flat surfaces and solid structural parts such as legs; *veneer* means it has a thin layer of veneer on top of a less refined wood. If a tag reads "cherry finish," it refers to the color only, not to the actual type of wood used.

You will need a table with two armchairs and at least two to four side chairs, depending on the size of your table. If your table is round or square, you may choose either all side chairs or all armchairs. You may also want a side piece for serving and storage.

Dining tables should be chosen according to the size and shape of the room. They are available in all styles, sizes, and shapes, including oval, rectangular, round, and square. An oval table will fit better in a smaller room; a rectangular, double-pedestal table seats the most people because it offers more flexible seating around the perimeter, whereas a table with a leg in each corner limits seating; a round or square table is best for a square room, or when a corner of a room is used for dining.

The most common sizes are:

- Oval   44 × 64 inches, seats four; with one leaf, seats six
- Rectangular 46 × 72 inches, seats six; with one leaf, seats eight; with two leaves, seats ten
- Round   42 to 48 inches, seats four; 54 to 60 inches, seats six
- Square   38 to 42 inches, seats four

Dining chairs should be chosen for comfort as well as style. They should also be sturdy because they must withstand much handling over the years to come. Those with padded seats or separate cushions should be covered in a fabric that is easy to clean.

Serving pieces such as a *buffet*, *credenza*, or *sideboard* are both decorative and practical for serving and storage in a more formal room. In an informal room, a *dry sink*, *huntboard*, or even a *chest of drawers* will serve the same purpose. If your room is narrow, look for one that is not too deep.

When you go out to shop, take a copy of your floor plan with you. If you do not have one, measure your room with a metal tape and draw it, using ¼-inch-scale graph paper and templates in the same scale. Keep in mind that you need three to four feet on each side of the table for chairs.

If you have already decided on carpet, fabric, paint, and wall covering, take your samples with you, too. Before you decide on fabric for your chairs, take home samples to study in the room at different times of the day and under natural and artificial light.

To determine quality:

- Check the grain and finish for consistency.
- Check that table leaves fit well.
- Check that drawers fit well and glide easily.
- Check that doors open and close easily.
- Check the manufacturer's warranty.

Coordinating Your Patterns

The basic rule when choosing your china, silver, and crystal is to choose two patterned and one plain *or* two plain and one patterned. In other words, you may choose plain white or ivory china with a simple gold or platinum band and combine it with ornamented silver and cut crystal, *or* you may choose china with an overall pattern and combine it with plain silver and plain crystal.

Before you make your final choices, there are a few things you should take into consideration. The background of your dining room will dictate the formality of your table, whether the room is decorated in a definite period or a combination of furniture styles. It will also suggest your choice of colors and patterns.

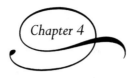

STARTING WITH YOUR CHINA

China is the focal point of the table, just as the table itself is the focal point of the room. The pattern should be chosen according to the formality of the room. It should also accent the color scheme and complement the style and lines of the furniture.

FORMAL

- China, translucent
- Porcelain, translucent

SEMI-FORMAL

- China
- Porcelain
- Earthenware including creamware

INFORMAL

- China
- Porcelain
- Earthenware including delftware, faience, ironstone, majolica, and stoneware.
- Woodenware

There are several considerations in selecting a china pattern: *color, pattern, shape,* and *finish.*

The *color* of formal china is white or ivory, embellished with gold or silver. For a semi-formal or informal room, a wide variety of colors may be used from plain white or ivory to a one-color or multicolored pattern to set or accent the color scheme of the room.

The *pattern* for a formal room should be subtle so as not to detract from fine furnishings and fabrics, such as white or ivory with gold or silver rococo or neoclassic motifs. For a semi-formal or informal room, a pattern that coordinates with the fabric and wallpaper in the room may be used.

The *shape* may be either rim, coupe, rectangular, or square. The rim shape complements contemporary, traditional, provincial, and country settings; the coupe, rectangular, and square shapes complement modern settings.

The *finish* of the china should complement the texture and finish of the table. Fine-grained polished woods are complemented by smooth translucent china and porcelain; woods with some grain are complemented by opaque china.

Selecting China

The word "chinaware" was originally used to describe the fine ware imported by England from China. Eventually the word was shortened to "china." Today most department stores have a china section with everything from *china* and *porcelain* to *earthenware* and *stoneware.*

All china is ceramic, which means it is made from clay and baked, but there are many different types, and you should know something about each type before you decide on a pattern. After all, when you shop for an important dress, first you decide on the type of fabric you want. Then you buy the style that best suits the purpose of the dress.

China is made from a mixture of white clays fired at very high temperatures to form a completely nonporous, nonabsorbent ware. It is off white or ivory in color. *Fine china* is made of choice refined clays. *Bone china* has all the qualities of fine china with bone ash added to the clay to make it white and translucent.

Porcelain differs from china only in the manufacturing process. It is slightly whiter than bone china and may be either translucent or opaque depending on the weight. The two are so similar the terms are used interchangeably. *Semiporcelain* is halfway between china and earthenware in composition and durability and is always opaque.

Earthenware is also opaque. It is made from coarser clay and baked at lower temperatures so it is porous and chips more easily than china, which is fired at higher temperatures. However, since at high temperatures most colors tend to change or fade, there are certain colors and patterns that are possible only in earthenware.

Creamware is a fine earthenware that is fired at a higher temperature. Although it is opaque, it is lighter in weight and looks similar to porcelain. It is usually a light cream color with molded or reticulated borders, but it is sometimes transfer printed.

Ironstone is a stronger type of earthenware made with the addition of china stone and fired at a higher temperature. Like other types of earthenware, it is also opaque and may be either light or heavy in weight. It is made in a wide variety of period styles and is usually all white with raised border designs.

Dutch Delft, *English delftware*, *French faience*, and *Italian majolica* are also types of earthenware. The French and Italian ware are decorated in bright colors, while Dutch Delft and English delftware are usually blue and white. Most of the English patterns are a little more formal than the Dutch.

Stoneware looks like earthenware but has the durability of china. It is heavier in appearance, which makes it much less formal. Some stoneware has a smooth finish that makes it look more like china, while some stoneware has an orange-peel texture.

Freezer-to-oven-to-table ware may be made of either porcelain or stoneware depending on the manufacturer. It is suitable for storing, baking, or microwaving, and also for serving.

There are several different ways a plate may be decorated. The skill and workmanship involved affects the price. For every color added, there is a separate firing in the kiln, so a plain white plate will cost much less than a decorated one. All techniques are used for every kind of ceramics, from porcelain to earthenware.

A *decal* is used to decorate most dinnerware made today. It is a design printed on a special paper, and comes in different parts and pieces that have to be matched very carefully. Even though it involves much handwork, it is the least expensive.

A *hand painted* design is the most expensive. When a plate is entirely painted by hand, you will see slight variations in the colors and designs. Colored or gold or platinum lines added to a design are also hand painted.

A *hand-filled* design is applied with a decal and the colors filled in by hand. This technique is less costly than a design that is completely hand painted.

A *printed* design is made on an engraved copper plate, transferred to a special paper, and then applied to the ware. This technique is used for allover patterns like Blue Willow. It is expensive because a different copper plate is needed for every size piece in the pattern.

A *platinum or gold rim* is usually applied to the surface of a plate after it has been glazed. It is painted on with a brush and then the plate is fired again in the kiln. After it is baked, it is polished to bring out its natural luster. Sometimes the plate is then dipped into an acid bath to etch a design into the metal, which is much more expensive than a plain rim of gold or platinum.

A design may be applied either before or after a plate is glazed. If a pattern is *under the glaze*, it is sealed and will not wear off but if it is *over the glaze*, it will not be dishwasher safe. However, the colors that may be used under the glaze are also limited because some colors change or fade from the high temperature at which a glaze is fired.

China sold in this country comes from all over the world, including England, France, Germany, Italy, Scandinavia, and also Japan.

England has been famous for bone china since the mid-eighteenth century when Josiah Spode developed the formula. Spode and Wedgwood are the leading companies. The early Spode motifs reflect a strong Chinese influence, while the Wedgwood patterns and shapes are more classic.

Germany has been famous for porcelain since the early eighteenth century when Johann Fredrich Bottger developed the formula, and the first porcelain factory in Europe was started at Meissen. Many of the early patterns are still being made.

France is also famous for porcelain. Limoges, a town in France, and not a brand of china as some people think, is the heart of the French porcelain industry. Bernadaud and Haviland are made there.

Italy is best known for the fine china made by Richard Ginori, which was started in the mid-eighteenth century. It is the only large china company in Italy.

Scandinavia is known for the porcelain made by Royal Copenhagen of Denmark, Arabia of Finland, and Rorstrand of Sweden. The designs of each company are unique and unmistakable.

Japan is the largest single producer of china in the world. Although Japan makes china with authentic Japanese designs, it also adapts the best designs of other countries at much less cost. The best known company is Noritaki.

American china is as varied as the Japanese. Lenox and Pickard are our proudest examples. Lenox, founded in the late nineteenth century by Walter Scott Lenox in New Jersey, has made fine china for the personal use of our presidents since 1918. Pickard, which was started in the mid-twentieth century, makes china for the diplomatic reception rooms of the White House and for the U.S. embassies and consulates worldwide.

Other American companies include Homer Laughlin, which is best known for Fiesta; Franciscan, which makes earthenware; Pfaltzgraff, which makes stoneware; and many smaller companies that specialize in different types of earthenware and stoneware.

There are so many patterns from which to choose that you really should spend some time studying manufacturer's catalogs and visiting their Web sites. A few hours doing this will help you develop an eye for *what goes with what*. You will find that most china patterns reflect design periods, as does furniture. Many patterns are updated versions of patterns that were introduced during a great furniture period and have names such as Federal Gold, Provincial Garden, and French Countryside.

Shopping for China

China is usually sold by the *place setting*, and also in *open stock*, which means that individual pieces of a pattern may be bought separately. It does not mean that a store will always have every piece, but will special order it for you as long as the manufacturer is still making it. Popular patterns are made for twenty years or more; others for only a few years.

China is also sold in *closed sets*. That means you have to buy the entire group of dinnerware in that pattern, packaged by the manufacturer. The most common sets today are for six, eight, or twelve place settings. There are also services for four called *starter sets*, which are usually only available in more casual china.

If you have a large family or entertain often, you will need eight to twelve place settings for formal and semi-formal dinners. You will also need some serving pieces. For everyday use, you may also want a different set from the rest of your china.

A five-piece place setting consists of a *dinner plate, salad plate, bread-and-butter plate*, and a *teacup and saucer*.

- The *dinner plate* is about 10½ inches in diameter and may also be used as a small platter or service plate.
- The *salad plate* is about 8 inches in diameter and is also used for

some desserts or as a small service plate.
- The *bread-and-butter plate* is about 6 inches in diameter and may also be used at cocktail parties for canapés and such.
- The *teacup* holds about 7 ounces and is also used for coffee at luncheons and informal dinners.

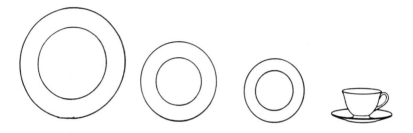

You will also need rim soup plates or cream soup cups and saucers, or both.

- The *rim soup* plate is about 9 inches in diameter and is the correct size for formal dinners.
- The *cream soup cup* and saucer is for cream soup but may be used for other soups as well.

For serving coffee you will need demitasse cups and saucers and after-dinner cups and saucers.

- The *demitasse cup* holds about 2 ounces and is used at formal dinners only.

- The *after-dinner cup* holds about 4 ounces and is used at semi-formal dinners.

Other pieces available in most patterns are the luncheon plate, the cereal dish, and the fruit saucer.

- The *luncheon plate* is 9 inches in diameter and is also used for the second course at dinner and for breakfast and late-evening entertaining.
- The *cereal dish* is 6 inches in diameter and may also be used as a small serving dish.
- The *fruit saucer* is 5 inches in diameter and may also be used for some desserts and for serving lemon wedges or pats of butter.

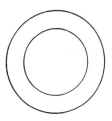 

Once you have all the pieces you need for dinner, you will want to add others. Extra teacups and saucers are a necessity. How many you need will depend on whether you have teas for thirty, or just a few. You will also need more plates for sweets. There are many other pieces you may need as you develop your social life. If you have dinner buffets for large groups, you will need more dinner plates. You may also need more luncheon plates for luncheon buffets and late-evening entertaining.

A five-piece serving set consists of a *cream pitcher, sugar bowl with cover, open vegetable dish,* and a *14-inch oval platter.*

- The *cream pitcher* holds about 6 ounces and is in scale with the teacup.
- The *sugar bowl* may be open or covered and is also in scale with the teacup.
- The *open vegetable* dish may be either round or oval.
- The *14-inch oval platter* will hold a roast with garniture for four to six people.

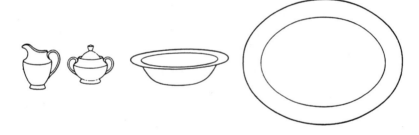

You will also need some more platters, a *gravy boat,* and a *coffeepot* and *teapot*.

- The *16-inch oval platter* will hold a roast with garniture for six to eight people.
- The *12-inch round platter* is used for chops and may also be used for cake, pies, and pastries.
- The *gravy boat* is either attached to a stand or has a separate saucer.
- The *coffeepot* and *teapot* come in standard sizes and in individual ones for breakfast.

Once you have the basic serving pieces, others may be added later on. You will need at least two or three more open vegetable dishes. You will also need a deep bowl for soft foods such as mashed potatoes and rice. There are many other pieces available. What you need will depend on what you serve. If you serve soup at the table, you will need a soup tureen. For holiday dinners, you will also need a 24-inch platter to serve a large ham or turkey.

Do not feel you need a complete set of your pattern because all the pieces will not be on the table at the same time. Some manufacturers have designed dinner services with coordinating motifs, plain borders on some, floral on others. You may also choose your dinner service in one pattern, dessert service in another pattern. Just remember, you may vary your pattern, but the quality must be consistent.

When you go out to shop, take a picture of your dining room furniture or the furniture you hope to have with you. Also take samples of your carpet, fabric, and wall covering. Your salesperson will help you put together a few place settings so you may see how the repetition of color and design will look around the table. It is important to do this because your china will be the focal point of your table, *setting after setting.*

To determine quality:

- Check that the plate lies flat on the table.
- Check that the cup handle is easy to hold.
- Check that the cup fits firmly in the saucer.
- Check that the pattern is sold in open stock.
- Check the manufacturer's warranty.

Caring for Dinnerware

Most dinnerware is dishwasher safe, but fine china that is decorated with gold or platinum should be hand washed and hand dried. In either case, use a soft paper towel to scrape off remaining food. Never use an abrasive cleanser. If coffee or tea has dried in the cups, use borax and a soft towel to remove stains. Remove scratches from cutlery by rubbing the marks gently with toothpaste.

When washing fine china by hand, line the sink with a towel or use a plastic basin or rubber mat. Do not use a rubber mat with dinnerware decorated with gold or silver. There may be a reaction between the rubber and precious metals that will leave a brown mark. Also, be sure to remove your rings. Diamonds and other gemstones will scratch almost any surface. Use a mild dishwashing liquid, rinse dishes in warm water, and air-dry them in a rubber-coated dish rack.

Never put dinnerware that is decorated with gold or platinum in a microwave. There may be a reaction that may cause sparks and leave the decoration mottled or pitted and also damage the microwave. Instead, dinnerware decorated with precious metals should be warmed in the plate-warming cycle of a dishwasher or in a standard oven for five to ten minutes at 150°F.

Fine earthenware should be washed the same way as fine china. Some hand-painted dinnerware will not withstand machine washing. If you are not sure about your dinnerware, follow the manufacturer's instructions. Most manufacturers include instructions, but you may also call the manufacturer's consumer number and ask for instructions.

Glassware and plasticware are completely dishwasher safe. Dishwasher detergent will not hurt the finish and the pattern will not wash off. Just do not scrub the surface with an abrasive cleanser or pad.

Storing Dinnerware

Store fine china with separating pads between plates, or use paper towels or napkins. Never stack cups but place them individually on a shelf, hang them on hooks, or put them on cup racks. Store fine china that is not used often in storage cases. Quilted or padded, zippered cases with protector pads are sold at department stores and specialty stores and through mail order catalogs.

Stack earthenware, stoneware, glass, and plastic dinnerware without pads in between, but do not slide one on the other. Place them one at a time on top of each other.

Store dinnerware that you use more often in a convenient place. Put those items that you use less often on top shelves. If storage space is limited, use cabinet organizers. There are racks available for plates, cups, and platters that are covered with a coating that will protect your dinnerware from nicks.

DECIDING ON YOUR SILVER

Silverware is like jewelry for your table. The pattern should be chosen as carefully as you would an accessory for your most important dress. It should complement your china pattern and also the style and lines of the furniture in the room.

FORMAL

- Silver
- Vermeil

SEMI-FORMAL

- Silver
- Silver plate
- Stainless steel
- Stainless steel with contrasting handles such as porcelain or pewter

INFORMAL

- Silver
- Silver plate
- Stainless steel
- Stainless steel with contrasting handles such as bamboo, bone, horn, Lucite, plastic, pewter, and wood.

There are several considerations in selecting your silver: *color, pattern, shape,* and *finish.*

The *color* of the metal should complement the china pattern. Gold complements china decorated with gold; silver complements china decorated with platinum; silver decorated with gold complements either metal.

The *pattern* of silverware should complement the design of the china pattern. Silver decorated with rounded motifs complements china decorated with rounded motifs; silver decorated with straight lines complements china decorated with straight lines.

The *shape* of the handle should also complement the shape of the china. Silver with curved handles complements china in the rim shape; handles with straighter lines complement china in the coupe or square shape.

The *finish* of the metal should complement the texture of the china. Metal with a bright finish complements china with a smooth finish; a matte finish complements china that is heavier in texture.

Selecting Silver

The word "silver" is a generic word commonly used to describe all types of silverware. Most department stores also have a silver section with everything from *sterling* and *vermeil* to *silver plate, gold plate, pewter,* and *stainless steel.*

Sterling silver is expensive, but nothing has the look or feel of sterling. The more you use it, the more beautiful it will become, developing a patina that only comes with age and use. With reasonable care, it will last a lifetime and may be handed down for generations.

The price of a sterling silver place setting may be two or three times more than your china place setting. Therefore, the selection of your silver is the one you will want to take the most time with. You will be living with it for a long, long time. Some experts recommend choosing your silver pattern first, but it should be chosen in relation to your china pattern and your dining room furniture or the furniture you plan to have.

In order to be called sterling, it must be made of a mixture of 92.5 parts pure silver to 7.5 parts copper. The standard is regulated by law, which is important because sterling silver is valuable as a material itself. It is one of the most precious metals, second only to gold. When you buy sterling silver, most of the price is in the material. While design and workmanship add to the cost, the amount of metal used and the weight of each piece is the main factor.

Silver may be *engraved*, *embossed*, or *chased*. An *engraved* pattern is incised or cut into the metal with a sharp tool. An *embossed* design is punched up from the back to create a raised design. A *chased* design is traced onto the metal with a blunt-edged tool. Another technique combines a chased design with an embossed design and is called *repoussé*. First the design is chased on the top, then the chased areas are punched up from the back. Most repoussé is highly ornate and is usually used in an allover design.

Vermeil is sterling silver plated with 24-karat gold and is even more expensive than sterling. It is available in a wide variety of patterns. Tiffany's revived it and Jackie Kennedy popularized it when she used it for state dinners during her husband's presidency.

Your other choices include *silver plate*, *gold plate*, *pewter*, and *stainless*.

Silver plate is made of a base metal of nickel silver plated with 99 percent pure silver. The most used items, such as forks and spoons, are double plated on the areas of greatest wear. There are almost as many patterns to choose from as sterling, but it is much less expensive.

Gold plate is made of a base metal of copper or steel plated with 24-karat gold. Good quality gold plate is about the same price as good silver plate. However, it is not available in as many patterns as silver plate.

Pewter is made of tin alloyed with antimony and copper. The blades, bowls, and tines are made of stainless steel. Most patterns are available in a bright or satin finish. Better quality pewter may cost almost as much as sterling.

Stainless steel is an alloy of steel, chrome, and nickel. It is available in a wide variety of patterns, and in some patterns there is a choice of bright or matte finish. Better quality stainless may cost more than silver plate.

Unlike china or glassware, most silverware sold in this country is made here—most of it manufactured in the Middle Atlantic and New England states by such companies as Gorham, Kirk Stieff, Lunt, Reed & Barton, Towle, and Wallace. The industry developed in these states during the days of colonial silversmiths.

The first designs used by American silversmiths were of English and European origin. In the New England states, the influence was English, in New York it was Dutch, and the Huguenots' influence was felt wherever they settled. There were just a few basic styles: the plain designs of the Puritans and the more elaborate designs that were curved, fluted, and scrolled like the carvings on fine eighteenth-century furniture.

Beautiful furniture has always inspired the silversmith. If you study manufacturers' catalogs and visit their Web sites, you will be able to trace the influence of furniture styles on silver patterns. You will find patterns with names such as English Chippendale, French Provincial, and American Colonial. If your style is modern, you will also find many patterns from which to choose. Like modern furniture, modern patterns have clean lines with little or no decoration.

Shopping for Silver

Silver is sold by the place setting and also in open stock, so when you choose a silver pattern you may be sure you will always be able to get it. When a silver company "discontinues" a pattern, it just deactivates it.

Usually, once a year, all manufacturers take orders for inactive patterns. The way silver is made, it is easy for a manufacturer to continue a popular pattern because the original dies are preserved.

Department and specialty stores sell silver by the place setting and in open stock. Mail order catalogs sell silver by the place setting and also in sets of four, eight, and twelve. The sets for eight and twelve are often packaged with serving pieces in a hostess set.

Depending on how many place settings you have of your china, you will need at least eight to twelve place settings. You will also need some serving pieces and some hollowware. For everyday use, you might also want a set of easy-care stainless steel.

A five-piece place setting consists of a *fork*, a *salad fork*, a *knife*, a *soup spoon,* and a *teaspoon.*

- The *fork* is used with the knife for the main course.
- The *salad fork* is also used for some desserts.
- The *knife* is used for the main course at dinner and at lunch if meat is served.
- The *soup spoon* may also be used for some desserts.
- The *teaspoon* is used with the teacup and also for fruit and some desserts.

Before you decide on a pattern, there are several decisions you will have to make. One decision is the size of the knife and fork. The other decision is the type of soup spoon.

There are three sizes from which to choose: *dinner size, luncheon size,* and *place size.*

- The *dinner-size* knife and fork are about one-half inch longer than the place size.
- The *luncheon-size* knife and fork are about one-half inch shorter than the place size.
- The *place-size* knife and fork are in between the dinner size and the luncheon size.

The dinner-size knife and fork are in proportion to the dinner plate and balance the array of tableware needed for a formal, multicourse dinner. The luncheon size is in proportion to the smaller luncheon plate. If you have family holiday and special occasion dinners often, or entertain often, start with the dinner size. Add the luncheon size, which may also be used for the second course, later on.

There are two soup spoons from which to choose: the *place spoon* and the *cream soup spoon*.

- The *place spoon* has an oval bowl and is used for most soups and cereal, and also for some desserts.
- The *cream soup spoon* has a round bowl and may also be used as a ladle for dessert creams and sauces.

If you have rim soup plates, choose the place spoon; if you have cream soup cups and saucers, choose the cream soup spoon.

You will also need *butter spreaders* and *seafood forks*.

- The *butter spreader* is available with a flat handle or a hollow one and may also be used for other spreads.
- The *seafood fork* has three prongs and short tines and is used for crabmeat and shrimp cocktail.

If you have demitasse cups and after-dinner coffee cups, you will need *demitasse spoons* and *coffee spoons*.

- The *demitasse spoon* is smaller than the coffee spoon and in proportion to the demitasse cup and saucer.
- The *coffee spoon* is smaller than the teaspoon and in proportion to the after-dinner coffee cup.

Once you have the basic pieces needed for dinner, you will want to add other pieces. Additional teaspoons are a necessity, and if you have dinner buffets for large groups, you will need additional forks. For the time being, you may use teaspoons, place spoons, and salad forks for most desserts. Later on, you may want to add dessert spoons and forks. If you live in a warm climate, you will also want iced-beverage spoons. There are many other pieces you may find you need as time goes by. There is no prescribed list. It all depends on your lifestyle.

A five-piece serving set includes a *tablespoon*, a *pierced tablespoon*, a *cold-meat fork*, a *butter knife*, and a *sugar spoon*.

- The *tablespoon* is used to serve fruit and vegetables and may also be used for casseroles, potatoes, and rice.
- The *pierced tablespoon* is used for any fruit or vegetable served in its own juice.
- The *cold-meat fork* is used to serve any sliced meat, hot or cold, or chops.
- The *butter knife* may be used to cut pâtés and soft cheeses as well.
- The *sugar spoon* may also be used as a serving spoon for jellies, marmalades, and preserves.

You will also need a carving set and ladles in various sizes.

- The *carving set* includes a long two-prong fork, knife, and steel to sharpen the blade.
- The *cream sauce* ladle is used for cream sauces, cream dressings, and whipped creams.
- The *gravy ladle* is the basic serving ladle for gravies and sauces.
- The *soup ladle* is only needed if you serve soup at the table from a soup tureen.

Adequate serving pieces add to the comfort and convenience of your family and guests. What you need will depend on how you entertain and what you serve. Even if you only serve cake at birthday and anniversary dinners, you will need a cake knife and a cake server. You will also need a lemon fork and sugar tongs for serving tea. There are many other pieces you may want to add later such as an asparagus server, fish servers, berry spoon, cheese knife, and various cheese servers, to name a few.

If you already have your china, take a plate with you when you go to shop. Also take your carpet, fabric, and wall covering samples with you. Your salesperson will help you arrange different patterns with your plate so you will be able to see how they look together. If you are getting married, because of the high cost of silver, list all your choices but note that you want knives, forks, and spoons first. Other pieces may always be added over countless anniversaries, birthdays, and holidays.

To determine quality:

- Check that the knife has a good cutting edge.
- Check that the fork fits comfortably in your hand.
- Check that the tines are symmetrical and smooth.

- Check that the pattern is sold in open stock.
- Check the manufacturer's warranty.

Hollowware

In addition to your flatware, you will also need some hollowware unless your style is cottage, country, or modern, in which case, ceramics would be more in keeping with your decorating style. You most certainly will need coffee and tea services, and if you have large buffets, you will need at least one covered baker and one covered casserole or chafing dish. You will also need some trays. A round ten-inch tray is a good all-purpose tray to begin with. Later you may add some larger ones.

Monograms

If you decide to personalize your silver with an initial or monogram, your salesperson or bridal registrar will show you sketches of script and block styles and will help you choose the right style for your pattern. If you are Mary Ellen Smith, but are going to be Mary Ellen Jones, you will use the initials MSJ. The last initial is usually centered and flanked by the first and second initial and, depending on the design, the J may be larger. Or you may use the single initial J.

The placement of the monogram on the handle depends on how the fork is placed on the table and held in the hand. In the United States, the monogram is placed on the front of the handle. The exception is an overall pattern that does not have room on the front, in which case the monogram is placed on the back. In England and Europe, the monogram is always placed on the back of the handle.

Caring for Flatware

Sterling silver needs the most care, but if you use it and wash it often, it will need to be polished less often. Also be sure to rotate the pieces so that each piece is washed routinely. Wash or rinse silver as soon as possible after using it since some foods, such as eggs, mayonnaise, mustard, vinegar, and salt may cause tarnish. Use hot soapy water, and rinse in clear hot water. Do not use lemon-scented detergents or those that contain chlorides. Never wash sterling silver and stainless steel together as there may be a reaction that will pit the silver. Dry immediately with a soft cloth to prevent spotting.

Silver plate needs the same care as sterling. Vermeil is subject to dents and scratches and should also be hand washed. However, gold does not tarnish and does not stain. Pewter is a soft alloy and is also subject to dents and scratches and should be washed by hand too.

Stainless steel is the easiest to care for and is dishwasher safe. However, like silver, it may become discolored from some dishwasher detergents. Put spoons and forks in baskets with handles facing down and knives with blades facing down. Drying additives may be used to minimize water spots. Use rubbing alcohol or salad oil to remove stubborn water spots.

Storing Flatware

Store sterling sliver and silver plate in an airtight silver chest or protective bags made of tarnish-proof cloth. Do not store silverware loose in drawers that are opened frequently even if they are lined with tarnish-proof cloth as exposure to air will cause tarnish. Also do not store silverware directly on a wood surface as wood often contains acids that cause damage.

Storage bags, pouches, and rolls made of tarnish-proof cloth are available at department and specialty stores and through mail order catalogs. The cloth is also available by the yard. It is easy to cut to make liners for drawers and your own storage keepers.

A word of caution: count your silver before storing it to make sure a piece has not been thrown away by mistake during cleanup.

ADDING YOUR CRYSTAL

Crystal adds height, light, and sparkle to your place setting. The pattern should be chosen in relation to your china and silver patterns. It should complement the shape of your china and silver and also the lines of the furniture in the room.

FORMAL

- Clear crystal, plain or with gold or platinum rims
- Clear crystal, cut, cased, engraved or etched
- Colored crystal
- Iridescent crystal

SEMI-FORMAL

- Clear crystal, plain or simply cut
- Colored crystal, semi-opaque

INFORMAL

- Clear crystal, plain, uncut and undecorated
- Colored crystal, opaque
- Milk glass

The main considerations in choosing your crystal are *color*, *pattern*, *shape*, and *finish*.

The *color* of formal crystal is clear or lightly tinged with color. For a semi-formal or informal room, it may be clear or any color that accents the color of your china pattern or the color scheme of the room.

The *pattern* of your crystal should complement the pattern of your china. Crystal that is cut or etched complements formal china and porcelain; plain, undecorated crystal complements semi-formal and informal china patterns.

The *shape* of your crystal should complement the shape of your china and silver patterns. Stemware with a rounded bowl complements china and silver decorated with rounded motifs; flat-bottomed bowls with straight, flared sides complement china and silver decorated with straight lines.

The *finish* of the glass should complement the finish of your china and silver. Crystal that is light and highly polished complements china and silver with a smooth finish; stemware that is heavier in texture complements china and silver that is heavier and opaque.

Selecting Crystal

The word "crystal" comes from the Italian word *cristallo,* which means clear and transparent. It is a generic word commonly used to describe all types of glassware. Most department stores also have a crystal section with everything from *glass* to *crystal* to *crystalline.*

Glass is made from a mixture of sand, lime, soda, and potash. *Crystal* is made with the addition of 10 to 24 percent lead oxide. *Lead crystal* has 24 to 30 percent lead oxide. *Full lead crystal* has 30 to 33 percent lead oxide. The higher the lead content, the clearer the glass. *Crystalline* is made almost entirely with potash.

All types of glass may be *blown* or *pressed* into shape. *Blown* glass is the clearest glass and the most expensive. Until recently all fine glassware was hand blown. Now a few of the better-quality glass manufacturers use computers as blowers. *Pressed* glass may be made by hand or machine. It is heavier and simpler in design than blown glass.

You may choose from *cut, engraved, or etched* glassware, decorated with brushed or stamped gold or platinum, or plain clear or colored glass. *Cut* glass takes great skill to execute and is the most expensive glassware. A *cut* design is made with a wheel that makes shallow indentations, such as on the bowls of stemware. An *engraved* design is also made with a wheel and is used for intricate details such as a floral motif or for monograms. An *etched* design is traced onto glass and then etched out with acid.

Like china, glass may be *hand painted*, decorated with a *decal*, or it may be *silk-screened*. Painted glass is not dishwasher safe and the pattern will wear off after repeated washings. If any gold or silver is used, it will also peel and fade like it does with china.

Colored glass may be transparent, semi-opaque, or opaque. It may be formal, semi-formal, or informal, depending on the color and design. A colored glass usually costs more than a plain glass because more materials are used to make it.

Lustreware is another kind of glass in which chemicals are used to achieve an iridescent effect. Although the colors are sprayed on and are not part of the composition of the glass, they are colorfast. It is transparent and is used in formal settings only.

Milk glass and *opaline* are two types of nontransparent glassware. The whiteness of the chemical mixture used makes milk glass opaque. It is much less formal than clear glass and complements Early American or country settings. Also milky in appearance, opaline is semi-opaque and a little more formal. It comes in a wide variety of pastel colors and also in a deep aquamarine. It is hand blown and more expensive than milk glass, which is machine made. Most modern milk glass is made in this country and is pressed, while opaline comes from Europe, mostly Italy, and is blown.

Frosted glass has a matte finish unlike all other kinds of glassware and is almost always colored. The frosting will not wear off and the color will not fade in the dishwasher. Depending on the design and styling, frosted glass may be used in formal or semi-formal table settings. It is more expensive than clear glass because of a more costly production technique.

Cased glass is one layer of glass blown right over another. The inside layer is clear; the outside colored. Designs are created by cutting through from one layer to another. It is expensive because it is difficult to make and requires great skill.

Glassware is made in almost every country, but certain countries are famous for producing different kinds of glassware.

England and *Ireland* are the most famous for cut crystal. The patterns are usually quite traditional in design and will coordinate very well with most English bone china. *Waterford* is the most famous.

France is famous for all types of crystal including clear, cut, cased, colored, and frosted. *Baccarat, Saint-Louis,* and *Lalique* are well known for design and quality.

Germany is known as one of the most versatile glass producers in the world. The Germans make traditional lead crystal patterns and also a plain blown glass that is very modern. *Spieglelau* is the best known.

Sweden is probably the most famous for the shape of the glass. *Kosta Boda* and *Orrefors* are the most well known of the Swedish glassmakers.

Italy is the leader in colored glassware. The island of Murano, off the coast of Venice, is the center of the industry and was also its birthplace. *Salviati* and *Venini* are both famous for their colored glass.

All countries make glassware of some type. Those just mentioned are the leading producers of specific types. A good deal of glass on the market comes from the *Czech Republic, Hungary,* and *Slovenia. Japan* is slowly entering the industry but does not make as much glass as it does dinnerware.

All types of glassware are made here but the most typically American is pressed glass. No other country produces as much pressed glass as the United States. The American glass industry was slow to develop because of British law that forced the colonies to import glass from England and Ireland. After the American Revolution, Casper Wistar started the first glassworks in New Jersey, followed by "Baron" Stiegel in Pennsylvania, and John Frederick Amelung in Maryland, with glassworkers brought over from Germany, England, Ireland, and Italy.

By the nineteenth century, the New England Glass Company, started by Deming Jarves in Massachusetts, was in full operation. While the glassware made by the company did not compare with the English and Irish imports, Jarves invented pressed glass, which was the beginning of the glass industry in America.

Libbey, which has been making glass for 180 years, began when William L. Libbey bought the New England Glass Company. A few years later, the company revolutionized glassmaking with the development of the first automatic glassmaking machine. Today the company makes both pressed and blown glass by machine.

L. E. Smith, which was started in the early twentieth century, still makes pressed glass by hand. The company is known for Depression glass reproductions and also for milk glass. You may want to visit the factory and see how it is made if you are in the vicinity of Mount Pleasant, Pennsylvania.

If you study manufacturers' brochures and visit their Web sites, you will find a wide variety of glassware from which to choose, from formal tall-stemmed crystal to informal low-footed glassware.

Shopping for Crystal

Department and specialty stores sell crystal in open stock. The term "open stock" in glassware means the same thing as it does in dinnerware, but glassware patterns are harder to find over the years than dinnerware. The reason is that there are fewer companies that have an interest in keeping certain patterns. However, it is much easier to find similar, or almost identical, patterns than to find matching china patterns.

Some stores price glassware by the set but you may always buy a single piece. If you choose a closed set, make sure it has more of each size than you really need. Some glassware is sold in sets and open stock, which is much safer.

Depending on how many place settings you have of your china and silver, you will need eight to twelve place settings of crystal. You will also need some serveware and barware. For everyday use, you may also want a set of inexpensive, multipurpose glassware.

A three-piece place setting consists of a *water goblet*, a *wine glass*, and a *champagne glass*, either flute or saucer.

- The *water goblet* is the largest glass and holds from 10 to 12 ounces.
- The *wine glass* is a smaller version of the water goblet.
- The *champagne flute* has a long narrow bowl, a shape that allows the bubbles to rise slowly, and is preferred by the connoisseur.
- The *saucer champagne* is shorter and shallower, but twice as wide, and may also be used for seafood cocktail and sorbet.

A wine connoisseur will say you need different glasses to bring out the bouquet and flavor of wine. If you plan to serve wine often, you should consider the different shapes and sizes. However, it is perfectly acceptable to have just one size wine glass. In fact, sometimes there is only one size available in a stemware pattern. In the United States, manufacturers make a red wine glass only. English and European manufacturers make a red wine glass, a white wine glass, a Rhine wine glass, and a sherry glass.

- The *red wine glass* holds eight to ten ounces and is used for all red wines except port and sherry.
- The *white wine glass* holds six to eight ounces and is used for all white wines except Rhine wine.
- The *Rhine wine glass* is similar to the white-wine glass but has a long stem and a shorter rounder bowl.
- The *sherry glass* holds four to six ounces and may also be used for other aperitifs and for dessert wines.

A wine connoisseur will also say wine should be served in a clear glass that will not distort the color of the wine. Colors like red, dark blue, and dark green will make red wine look muddy. Colored glass is acceptable for white wine, but clear glass is more adaptable. It complements any china pattern and will not detract the eye from a fully appointed table setting. If you really like colored glass, combine it with clear glass. For a more formal table, combine a colored champagne flute with a clear water goblet and wine glass. A colored water goblet may be combined with a clear wine glass in a less formal table setting.

Even though cocktails and cordials are not served at the table, these glasses are considered part of your stemware.

- The *cocktail glass* is shorter than the average wine glass and has a wider opening.
- The *cordial glass* usually comes in 1-ounce and 2-ounce sizes and is used for liqueurs and brandy.

These are the only glasses you really need in your expensive stemware. If you live in a warm climate, you may want to add footed iced beverage glasses. You may also want juice glasses later on, but these really do not have to match your stemware. If you have overnight guests or entertain at Sunday brunch often, you may use your white-wine glasses for juice.

It is best to choose your china pattern and your silver pattern first because your crystal will pull the entire place setting together. If you already have your china and silver, take a dinner plate and one place setting of your silver with you when you shop. Also, take a sample of your carpet, fabric, paint, and wall covering with you. Your salesperson will then be better able to help you choose a pattern.

To determine quality,

- Check that the base lies flat on the table.
- Check that the rim is even and smooth.
- Check that the bowl is free of imperfections.
- Check that the pattern is sold in open stock.
- Check that there is a manufacturer's warranty.

Barware is available in most patterns and includes highballs and tumblers in various sizes for drinks served on the rocks and for old-fashioneds. Some patterns also have ice buckets. However, if you have large informal gatherings often, you may want a less expensive set of multipurpose barware.

Serveware includes water pitchers and wine decanters and is also available in most patterns. You will need at least one water pitcher and one decanter for red wine. Later on, you may want to add decanters for whiskey and brandy.

Caring for Crystal

An easy way to remove product labels from new glassware is with hot air from a hair dryer. Use nail polish remover and a soft cloth to remove any gummy residue. Before washing new decanters or pitchers, fill with a solution of 50 percent lemon juice or vinegar and 50 percent water. Let stand for twenty-four hours, then empty and rinse with warm water. This will remove any residue from production or shipping.

Wash crystal in mild soap flakes or with a small amount of liquid detergent as recommended by the manufacturer. Use a faucet guard or nozzle and line the sink with a towel or use a plastic basin or rubber mat. Do not use a rubber mat if your crystal is decorated with gold or platinum as there may be a reaction between precious metals and rubber. Also be sure to remove your rings before you begin. Dry your crystal gently with a soft, lint-free cloth. Take special care when drying crystal decorated with gold or platinum. Wait until it has cooled down before wiping dry. When drying stemware, do not wipe the bowl while twisting the stem in the opposite direction since this may cause the stem to snap off.

Hard water may leave mineral deposits on your crystal. These deposits may be removed with vinegar and a soft cloth. You may also add vinegar to the water when hand washing your crystal to remove persistent spots. To remove film buildup from crystal containers, use a vinegar or lemon juice and water solution and let stand three to four hours before washing. If you are not able to reach inside a decanter or water pitcher, add uncooked rice to the solution and shake to clean the inside walls. Then empty and rinse with warm water.

Storing Crystal

Store crystal right side up. Standing crystal upside down may cause the rims to chip. Only store crystal that is completely dry and cool because, when glass is damp or warm, moisture will collect on the surface and form a film that is hard to remove. Also do not stack highballs or old-fashioned glasses as they may stick together.

Store crystal that is not used often in storage cases. Covered, zippered cases fitted with adjustable dividers are sold at department and specialty stores and also through mail order catalogs. Or keep the original boxes and repack until the next time you need them.

Chapter 7

FINISHING WITH YOUR TABLE LINENS

Table linens provide the background for your finished table setting. The fabric you use should complement the degree of formality of the room. It should also accent or set the color scheme and may also establish a definite theme and change the look of the table for different seasons.

FORMAL

- Formal textures, such as damask, moiré, and strié
- Lace, including appliqué and cutwork
- Organdy, appliquéd or embroidered

SEMI-FORMAL

- Cotton and linen prints, such as florals, including botanicals, chinoiserie, and Jacobean; toiles, either floral or scenic; plaids and stripes
- Cotton and linen solids

INFORMAL

- Cotton prints including small-scale florals and fruits; paisleys and paisley stripes; checks, plaids, and stripes; and thematics
- Cotton solids including burlap, denim, duck, and woven textures

The main considerations in choosing your linens are *color*, *pattern*, *shape*, and *finish*.

The *color* of formal dining is white or ivory. For a semi-formal or informal occasion or room, a wide variety of colors may be used from white and ivory to any color that coordinates with your china and the color scheme of the room.

The *pattern* used for a formal dinner should be subtle and not detract from the array of tableware needed, such as a white-on-white damask or fine white cotton or linen. For semi-formal or informal dining, a cotton or linen tablecloth, or place mats or runners in white, ivory, or a solid color or a pattern to coordinate with the wallpaper and fabric in the room may also be used.

The *shape* of your table linens depends on the shape of your table. A round table needs a round tablecloth and round or shell-shaped place mats; an oval table is best with an oval cloth and oval place mats. A rectangular table requires an oblong cloth and rectangular place mats.

The *finish* of the fabric should complement the texture of the tableware used. Fabric with a smooth, shiny finish complements translucent china and porcelain; fabric with some texture and a matte finish is better with opaque china and earthenware.

Selecting Table Linens

The words "table linens" are commonly used for tablecloths, place mats, runners, and napkins, even though they may not be linen. Tablecloths and napkins are made in everything from *cotton* and *cotton blends* to *linens,* and place mats from *plastic* to *straw* to *wood.*

Linen and *cotton* are the preferred choices. Both are made from strong, natural fibers that are often blended with each other or with other fibers. A blend of linen and cotton is long wearing and less expensive than pure linen; a cotton and polyester blend is easy to care for, but does not have the feel of a fabric made with all natural fibers.

Linen is made from flax, a fiber that comes from the stalk of the blue-flowered plants of the genus *Linum* that grow in the cooler climates of Europe. The finest flax is grown in the fields of Flanders in Belgium. It may be finely woven into smooth lustrous formal textures or loosely woven into less-formal textures.

Cotton is made from the boll that comes from the flowers of the cotton plant, which grows best in hot, humid climates. The finest variety is grown in the Nile delta of Egypt. It is the most versatile of fibers and may be woven plain or in a wide variety of patterns, textures, and weights from formal to informal.

Plain linens are often decorated with an *appliqué, cutwork,* or *embroidery,* inset and trimmed with *lace* or have a *hemstitch* border. An *appliqué* is a precut decoration that is made separately and then sewn or embroidered onto the cloth. A *cutwork* design is openwork in which the design is formed by cutting away fabric from a stitched outline. A *lace* inset or trim includes various types of openwork made with a pin or needle and thread. A *hemstitch* is a row of ornamental stitching on or near the hemline.

Patterns are *woven* or *printed*. A *woven* design is made up of fibers woven into the fabric. A *printed* design is printed on the already woven fabric. It may be *block printed, screen-printed,* or *roller printed.* A *block* print is done by hand, using hand-cut wood blocks, each of which prints one color and a certain section of a design at a time. A *screen* print is also done by hand, but the color is applied through a stencil cut on a silk screen. A *roller* print is a design etched on a copper roller and run off in volume, so it is the least expensive.

Most of the finer linens sold in this country are imported from Europe. *France* is known for the fine hand-embroidered linens made by Porthault that are sold here and also for damasks sold by Yves Delorme. *Italy* is known for the damasks made by Frette and Pratesi that are sold in their stores here.

There are several American companies that also sell European-made linens: Anichini imports linens from Italy; Braun and Leron from Italy, France, and Portugal; Schweitzer from France and Italy; and Gracious Style from Belgium, England, Ireland, France, and Italy.

Patterns for table linens are also adapted from eighteenth-century furniture. If you study manufacturers' catalogs and visit their Web sites, you will find formal damasks with classic rococo and neoclassic designs, and numerous other patterns, including French toiles, Scottish paisleys, and country florals of every type.

Shopping for Table Linens

Department and specialty stores sell tablecloths and matching napkins, which may be bought separately or as a set of six to twelve. Place mats are sold in sets including napkins, or by the individual mat with or without matching napkins. Runners are sold individually with matching place mats and napkins sold separately.

You will need at least one tablecloth of fine fabric with matching napkins for formal dinners and eight to twelve place mats and napkins for luncheons and semi-formal dinners. For everyday use, you will also need at least two easy-care tablecloths and eight to twelve place mats, with matching or contrasting napkins.

Tablecloths should be selected according to the height, shape, and size of the table. There is no set rule but the tablecloth should have a drop of ten to twelve inches. A longer cloth would be uncomfortable; a shorter cloth would be out of proportion. At a sit-down dinner, the cloth should rest on the diner's lap. For a buffet table or a tea table, the drop may be longer. For a wedding reception when the table is raised on a dais, the cloth should skim the floor.

The most common sizes are:

- Oblong 70 × 90 inches
  70 × 108 inches
  70 × 126 inches
  70 × 144 inches
- Oval 70 × 90 inches
  70 × 108 inches
- Round 70 inches
  90 inches
- Square 52 inches

If you plan to use one or more table leaves at different times, you will need more than one size tablecloth. Also a table with leaves will often change shape as well as size. For example, a round table becomes oval and a square table becomes oblong, so you will need more than one shape as well as more than one size.

A *table pad* should be used to protect the table, soften sounds, and keep the tablecloth in place. A folding pad made of felt on one side and a waterproof material on the other side may be custom made to fit the table, including the leaves, and ordered through furniture or department stores or by mail. Fabric padding is also available by the yard and may be cut to fit the table and finished with an elastic band.

Place mats may be used for every occasion except the most formal dinner or tea. They are the most versatile of all the table coverings and are available in a wide variety of colors, fabrics, patterns, sizes, and shapes. The size of the place mat should be large enough to hold the entire place setting. An oval or rectangular placemat should range in size from twelve to fourteen inches deep and from sixteen to eighteen inches wide; a round placemat should be approximately fifteen inches in diameter.

Table runners may be used for decoration or as place mats. Placed in the center of the table, one runner may be used with matching place mats on each side, or two or more may be crossed over each other and used as place mats for four or more people. Runners should be about twelve to sixteen inches wide and either fit the length of the table or have a drop of about twelve inches. If you want to cross two runners and you have an oblong or oval table, you will need two sizes: a longer one to fit the length of the table and a shorter one to fit the width of the table.

Napkins are available in a wide variety of sizes. The large twenty-four-inch formal dinner napkin is not widely used. A smaller napkin is more comfortable, in better proportion to the size of place mats, and is easier to fold.

The most common sizes are:

- Dinner napkins—18 to 22 inches square
- Lapkins—18 × 20 inches
- Luncheon napkins—15 to 17 inches square
- Tea napkins—12 inches square
- Cocktail napkins—9 inches square, or 4 × 6 or 6 × 9

When shopping, keep in mind that napkins used for formal settings should match the cloth. In the case of lace or organdy, use napkins of fine cotton trimmed with lace or appliquéd with organdy. For semi-formal settings, the napkins should match or blend but never contrast in color and rarely in texture with the table covering; for informal settings, the napkins may match, blend, or contrast in color and texture with the table covering.

Once you have a basic wardrobe for a well-dressed table, you will want to add to it. Extra napkins are essential. If you have teas for thirty, you will also need tea napkins that match or contrast with your formal tablecloth. You may also need a smaller tea cloth for serving tea to a few friends from a small table in your living room. A good supply of cocktail napkins is also needed for serving before-dinner drinks and for larger cocktail parties. If you have occasional overnight guests, you may also want one or two place mats and napkins to use on a breakfast tray that coordinate with your guest bedroom.

Before you set out to shop, measure the height, length, and width of your table. Take these measurements, a plate, a place setting of silver, your crystal, and your fabric and wall covering samples to the store with you. You will need them to coordinate your table linens with your tableware and the background of your dining room.

To determine quality:

- Check the color for consistency.
- Check the label for fiber content.
- Check the hem for workmanship.
- Check the manufacturer's warranty.

Monograms

You may decide to personalize your table linens instead of your silver. The placement of the initial or monogram on a tablecloth will depend on the pattern and design and how the table will be set. It may be placed in the middle of the cloth or diagonally on the corner just above the hem. The size of the lettering should be from 3½ to 5 inches, depending on the size of the cloth and where it is placed on the cloth.

The placement of the initial or monogram on the dinner napkin may be in the exact center, in the center of the side, or on the lower corner. If the napkin has a wide band, it may be placed on the band in the center of the side. An elongated monogram may be placed parallel to the hem on the corner of the napkin. A monogram is always placed on the corner of the luncheon napkin and the tea napkin. The size of the lettering on a dinner napkin should be from 2 to 3 inches, and for luncheon and tea napkins from 1½ to 2 inches.

Caring for Table Linens

Fine cottons, linens, and rayons should be washed in warm soapy water and rinsed twice. After they are washed and dried, dampen and iron them. Fold tablecloths in the middle but do not iron the fold. Every time you wash the cloth, move the fold a little bit to the right or left to keep it from wearing out in the middle. To bring out the design, iron embroidered or monogrammed linens on the wrong side. If you need to touch up wrinkles later it is easier to bring the ironing board to the table and slide the cloth onto the table as it is ironed. You may also iron the cloth right on the table over a heatproof pad, or use a steamer.

Storing Table Linens

The best way to store a tablecloth is folded in the middle, wrapped in acid-free tissue paper, and rolled around a cardboard tube. Another way is to hang it on a rod attached to the inside of a closet door. Napkins and place mats may be laid flat in a drawer with acid-free tissue paper in between. Runners may be hung on a rod.

Chapter 8

DRESSING YOUR TABLE

Before you set the table, you have to dress the table. The way you dress the table depends on the formality of the occasion and the room. A five-course dinner in an informal country room calls for less-formal linens than one in a formal traditional room.

Keep these guidelines in mind:

- *Tablecloths* unify the array of tableware needed for a multicourse dinner or large tea.
- *Place mats* should be placed flush on a table with a beveled edge or one inch from the edge on a table with a straight edge.
- *Runners* may be placed in the center of the table as decoration and used with matching place mats, or crossed over and used instead of place mats.
- *Napkins* should be placed to the left of the forks, about one inch from the edge of the table or in line with the lower edge of the place mat, with the open edge facing the forks.

Napkin Folds

Napkins should be folded into shape rather than pressed into shape. A folded napkin will lie on the lap more smoothly than a napkin with a crease. For a formal dinner, the napkin should be folded into a simple rectangle. At a luncheon or less formal dinner, the table setting is simpler and a more decorative fold may be used to add interest, such as a fan fold for a luncheon or a butterfly fold for an informal dinner.

- The *rectangle* fold may be placed on the left next to the forks, or on the service plate or dinner plate if the first course is not already in place. To make a rectangle, fold a large square napkin in half to make a long rectangle. Then fold the top half over the bottom half, and then fold again.
- The *fan* fold may be placed in the water goblet. To make a fan, fold the napkin in half. Then fold into accordion pleats, place the bottom edge in the goblet, and fan the top edge above the rim.
- The *butterfly* fold may be held with a napkin ring and placed to the left of the forks or on the dinner plate. To make a butterfly, accordion-pleat the napkin diagonally from corner to corner. Then fold the napkin in half at the center and insert in the napkin ring.

Formal Dinner

- Use a white or ivory damask, embroidered, or lace tablecloth for a formal room, or white or ivory cotton or linen for a semi-formal or informal room.
- Place a table pad underneath the tablecloth to keep the tablecloth in place.
- Match the dinner napkins to the tablecloth.

Semi-formal Dinner

- Use a white or ivory cotton or linen tablecloth.
- Use place mats in place of a tablecloth, if you like.
- Place a table pad underneath if you are using a tablecloth.
- Match or blend the napkins to the tablecloth or place mats.

Luncheon

- Use a white or ivory cotton or linen tablecloth, or for a more formal room use a cutwork cloth with or without a liner.
- Use white or ivory lace or organdy place mats for a formal room, or white or ivory cotton or linen or a pattern for a semi-formal or informal room.
- Use a runner down the center of the table with matching place mats, or cross runners for four or more guests.
- Put a table pad underneath if you are using a tablecloth.
- Match, blend, or contrast the napkins with the tablecloth or place mats.

Dinner Buffet

- Use a white or ivory damask tablecloth for a more formal room, or white, ivory, a color, or a pattern for a less formal room.
- Put a table pad underneath the tablecloth.
- Use dinner napkins for a formal sit-down buffet, or lapkins for an informal buffet when guests are sitting with plates on their laps.

Tea or Dessert Buffet

- Use a traditional white or ivory tea cloth for a formal or a semi-formal room, or white, ivory, or a color for an informal room.
- Use a tablecloth that skims the floor on a round table, if you are creating a Victorian tea table.
- Match, blend, or contrast the napkins with the tea cloth.

SETTING YOUR TABLE

The next step is learning how to use your table appointments. Tables are set in ordered positions for comfort and convenience. Carefully setting the table every day for your family will make it much easier when you entertain guests.

Keep these guidelines in mind:

- *China and silver* should be placed about one inch from the edge of the table; crystal just above the tip of the knife.
- *Bread-and-butter plates* are never used for a formal dinner of six or more courses.
- *Rim soup plates* are the correct size for a formal dinner; cream soup cups and saucers are used for a less formal dinner or luncheon.
- *Cups and saucers* are never part of a place setting.
- *Water goblets* are the only glasses in a luncheon setting.

Formal Dinner

- Place a service plate, which is removed from the table along with the first-course plate, at each place.
- Put the dinner plate on top of the service plate.
- Lay the dinner knife to the immediate right of the dinner plate with the cutting edge facing the plate.
- Lay the second-course knife to the right of the dinner knife.

82 WHAT GOES WITH WHAT

Formal Dinner

- Lay the soup spoon to the right of the knives.
- Lay the forks to the left of the dinner plate in the order of their use, from the outside in.
- Lay the second-course fork to the left of the dinner fork.
- Lay the salad fork to the right of the dinner fork.
- Set the water goblet just above the tip of the dinner knife.
- Set the red or white wine glass slightly to the right of the water goblet.
- Set the red and white wine glasses to the right of the water goblet, in that order, when serving both.
- Set the champagne glass behind the water and wine glasses, forming a triangle.
- Set individual salt and pepper shakers above each dinner plate.
- Place the napkin on the center of the top plate, or if the first course will be on the table when the guests are seated, place the napkin to the left of the forks.

- Make sure the monogram, if there is one, is at the lower edge of the rectangle or at the center facing the guest.
- Center a place card on each napkin or in a decorative holder.
- Put the centerpiece and candleholders on the table.
- Arrange demitasse service on a table in the living room.
- Place the dessert service on the table after it has been cleared.

Semi-formal Dinner

- Place the dinner plate on the table.
- Place the bread-and-butter plate at the upper left of the dinner plate.
- Lay the butter spreader horizontally across the top of the bread-and-butter plate.
- Lay the dinner knife to the right of the dinner plate.
- Lay the soup spoon to the right of the dinner knife if soup is the first course.

Semi-formal Dinner

- Lay the seafood fork to the right of the dinner knife, if seafood cocktail is the first course.
- Lay the forks to the left of the dinner plate in the order of use, from the outside in.
- Lay the salad fork to the left of the dinner fork, if the salad is served before the main course.
- Lay the salad fork to the right of the dinner fork, if the salad is served after the main course.
- Set the water goblet just above the dinner knife.
- Set the wine glass to the right of the water goblet.
- Set standard salt and pepper shakers between every two place settings.
- Place the napkin to the left of the forks.
- Put the centerpiece and candleholders on the table.
- Place the after-dinner coffee and dessert services on the table after it has been cleared.

Luncheon

- Place the luncheon plate about one inch from the edge of the table.
- Place the bread-and-butter plate at the upper left of the luncheon plate.
- Lay the butter spreader horizontally across the top of the bread and butter plate.
- Lay the luncheon knife to the right of the luncheon plate and the luncheon fork to the left of the plate.
- Lay the teaspoon to the right of the knife if a fruit cup is the first course.
- Lay the cream soup spoon to the right of the knife if serving cream soup as the first course.

SETTING YOUR TABLE 85

Luncheon

- Lay the salad fork to the left of the luncheon fork if the salad is served before the main course.
- Lay the salad fork to the right of the luncheon fork if the salad is served after the main course.
- Set the water goblet at the tip of the luncheon knife.
- Place the napkin to the left of the forks, on the luncheon plate, or fanned in the water goblet.
- Put the centerpiece on the table or a single flower or other decorative item at each place setting.
- Arrange sherry or wine service on a side piece.
- Place the coffee and dessert services on the table after it has been cleared.

Dinner Buffet

Arrange in the following order:

- Dinner plates (maximum of eight in each stack)
- Chafing dish with hot main course
- Second entrée
- Vegetable
- Salad
- Relish
- Breads
- Flatware
- Dinner napkins or lapkins, folded or wrapped around the flatware
- Coffee and dessert service along with glassware on a side table

Tea or Dessert Buffet

- Set the teapot with the creamer, sugar bowl, and plate of lemon slices on a tray at one end of the table.
- Set up a similar tray for coffee at the opposite end of the table.
- Place the cups on saucers with teaspoons and set near the coffee and tea.
- Stack the dessert plates or, if there is room, lay them out on the table or, if space is limited, place the plates on a side table.
- Place small folded napkins behind the plates together with the dessert forks.
- Put a small vase of flowers on each tray.
- Place sweets in the center of the table along with the appropriate serving pieces.

DECORATING YOUR TABLE

After you have set the table, you have to decorate the table. The accessories you choose will add the finishing touches to your table and reflect your personal taste. They should accent the color scheme and the style of the other table appointments.

Keep these guidelines in mind:

- *Decorations* should be suited to the style of the room and the occasion.
- *Proportion and scale* should complement the shape and size of the table.
- *Color, design, and texture* should complement the china pattern.
- *Containers* should be consistent with all the other table appointments.
- *Floral arrangements* should complement the shape and size of the container.

Decorations should suit the room and the spirit of the occasion for which the table is set, whether it is a dinner for guests or just for the family, a holiday buffet, or a luncheon for your committee members. An elaborate floral arrangement may be suitable for a special occasion, but a few flowers or a bowl of fruit is more suitable for a family dinner. When an elaborate decoration is used, it should not overpower the individual place settings. It should also look good from the view of all those seated at the table even though it does not have to look the same on all sides.

Proportion and scale should relate to the shape and size of the table. On a round table, the shape of the arrangement may be round, star shaped, or triangular, whereas the arrangement on a rectangular table should emphasize the length of the table.

When the seating arrangement is uneven and the decoration placed other than in the center, the decoration should be related to the space and have visual balance with the place settings. For example, in a setting for three or five people, one or two on each side, and one on one end, the decoration may be placed at the other end where it becomes the focal point for all those at the table. On a table placed in front of a window or against a wall with places set at each end and along one side, the other side may be used for an arrangement, lower in front of a window, higher against a wall.

Colors of the arrangement should complement the china pattern. If there are two or more colors in a china pattern, emphasize the dominant color. If your china is a one-color pattern such as blue and white, the arrangement may be in a contrasting color. Keep in mind that colors such as blue and violet look better in daytime than under artificial light, while reds and yellows look better under artificial light or candlelight.

Design of the arrangement should also complement your china pattern. The overall floral designs of early English patterns suggest a full arrangement of mixed flowers typical of that period, while chinoiserie designs suggest an arrangement that is Oriental in feeling.

Texture of the arrangement should complement your china pattern too. A heavier, more informal ceramic should have an arrangement that is heavier in color and form, while translucent china and porcelain require an arrangement that is more delicate in color and form.

Containers used for flowers should be consistent in texture and color, as well as quality with the other table appointments. If you use a ceramic container, it should be of the same texture as your plates: translucent china with translucent china, earthenware with earthenware. The color should also be consistent with the color or the background color of the plates: white with white, ivory with ivory. Likewise, if you use a metal container, it should also be consistent: silver with silver, pewter with pewter, bright metal with bright metal, matte metal with matte metal.

Floral arrangements should be kept in proportion to the shape and size of the container. For example, your arrangement should be one and one-half to two times the width of a low container or the height of a tall container. The height of an arrangement at a seated dinner should not be more than eighteen inches. A higher arrangement may be used on a buffet table, tea table, or wedding table, or any table at which the guests are not seated.

Fresh Flowers

Choose your flowers according to the formality and patterns and colors of your dining area. If you have a garden, cut your flowers the day before you arrange them. Morning is the best time to cut flowers because they have ample moisture then. Roses are said to last longer, however, if they are picked at midday. After you have picked the flowers, cut the stems under water on the diagonal about two inches from the bottom of the stem. Snap the stems of chrysanthemums and crush the stems of woody plants, such as forsythia, with a hammer. Remove pollen from lilies by pulling out the stamens to avoid discoloring the petals and staining your table linens. Then soak the stems in water overnight so they will harden.

When your garden is not in bloom, or if you do not have a garden, place your order with a florist as soon as your plans are completed because some flowers are not in stock all the time. Have them delivered in time for you to cut the stems and let them soak in water overnight. If you pick them up yourself, carry them home in a well-sealed, nonabsorbent paper or plastic bag, leaving enough room for an air pocket above their heads.

When arranging flowers, one type of flower and one color predominating is more visually pleasing. The darker the color, the lower it should be placed in an arrangement, while lighter colors are better placed on the sides and toward the top of the arrangement. To keep stems in place, use frogs or florist's foam blocks in the base of your container.

If you are making more than one arrangement, work on them at the same time. First arrange the predominating flower in each container. Then arrange the flowers that are secondary in importance. View the arrangement from all sides to make sure they all look the same.

Here are some suggestions:

Formal—gladiolas, lilies, orchids, roses, camellias, stephanotis, gardenias, magnolias
Semi-formal—carnations, chrysanthemums, peonies, roses, tulips
Informal—black-eyed Susans, cornflowers, daisies, daylilies, marigolds, poppies, primroses, sunflowers, zinnias

Potted Plants

In an informal room, a potted plant may be used as a centerpiece. Hide the pot by covering it with foil and wrapping it in fabric, or paint the pot and place on a metal, wicker, or wooden tray. A single plant is enough for a small round table, but three plants grouped together are better for a larger rectangular table.

There are many plants from which to choose. Flowering ones include amaryllis, begonias, daffodils, pansies, geraniums, iris, narcissus, poinsettias, and violets. Other plants such as ivy or herbs, small evergreen trees, and cactus also make attractive centerpieces.

Accessories

Think of accessories as objects for a still life and collect as many of them as you possibly can so that you will have a variety to work with when you decorate your table. You will need functional accessories such as candleholders and bowls and vases for flowers in a variety of shapes and sizes. In addition, you will want to have some decorative accessories to add height to the table when candles are not used, such as china or porcelain figurines for a more formal room or wooden folk art figures for an informal country room.

Candles

Candles are an important part of any table decoration. Collect them as you would accessories, but keep in mind they should be below or above eye level. Choose from tall tapers to low votives and tea lights to pillars in various sizes. Whatever the occasion, white or ivory is the best choice and blends with the background of most china patterns and also bare tabletops.

Creative Decorations

Creating your own decorations that can be used more than once from found or bought materials will save you time and money and give you personal satisfaction that no call or trip to your florist will. Your local supermarket or super store, crafts store, flower or gift shops, even the beach or woods, are good sources for seasonal materials that can be incorporated into centerpieces.

Start your collection with such items as artificial or dried fruits and vegetables, including turnips, gourds, Indian corn, pumpkins, nuts, and turning leaves in the fall. In winter, pick up bare branches, cranberries, pine cones, winter greenery, Christmas ornaments, and tiny white lights. Use bunches of asparagus, bird houses, colored eggs, Easter baskets and bonnets, garden statuary like stone rabbits, or even watering cans in spring. Summer decorations include beach pebbles, sea shells, starfish, sea oats, driftwood, miniature beach chairs, lighthouses, and sailboats.

Family Occasions

There are many other things that can be used to create centerpieces, such as ceramic or wooden art, picture frames, gift boxes, wrapping paper, and ribbon.

Here are some more ideas:

Anniversaries—the first layer of a wedding cake topped with the couple's wedding photograph
Birthdays—photograph of the birthday person at a young age, balloons, and confetti
Graduations—mortarboard and rolled-up diploma
Engagements—blow-up of the newspaper announcement

Holidays

When decorating for the holidays, try to avoid the obvious colors. For example, red and green are obvious choices for Christmas, but only use them if they fit with your color scheme. Other possibilities include silver and gold; burgundy, silver, and gold; pink or peach, green, silver, and gold; blue, silver, and gold. Another example is Valentine's Day. Instead of red, consider other versions of red, such as pink or peach, rose or coral.

Here are some other ideas:

CHRISTMAS SIT-DOWN DINNER

- Various sizes of wrapped gift boxes
- Small wrapped box at each place setting

CHRISTMAS DINNER BUFFET

- Various sizes of wrapped boxes used as risers for platters

NEW YEAR'S EVE BUFFET

- Noisemakers, horns, and party hats sprinkled with confetti

VALENTINE'S DAY SIT-DOWN DINNER

- Large heart-shaped box of chocolates
- Small heart-shaped box at each place setting

VALENTINE'S DAY TEA OR DESSERT BUFFET

- Tiered plate with small heart-shaped cakes or cookies
- Small heart-shaped cutouts scattered on the table

EASTER DAY SIT-DOWN DINNER

- Various sizes of wrapped boxes topped with nosegays
- Small wrapped box at each place setting
- Ceramic, stone, or wooden bunnies
- Colored or decorated eggs

MOTHER'S DAY

- Certificate of achievement listing the names of all her children

FATHER'S DAY

- Whatever represents his interests, such as golf balls and tees

HALLOWEEN

- Various sizes of pumpkins and gourds
- Small pumpkins at each place setting

THANKSGIVING

- Fresh fruit, including apples, oranges, bananas, and grapes
- All kinds of nuts and berries
- Ceramic or wooden pilgrims and Indians

Be creative and have fun when you decorate your table. This is your chance to add your personal flair and show how much you care about your guests.

Resource Guide

DINING ROOM FURNITURE—KITS

Bartley Collection
1-800-787-2800
www.bartleycollection.com
Eighteenth- and nineteenth-century Colonial American and Federal reproductions

Cohasset Colonials
1-800-288-2389
www.cohassetcolonials.com
Eighteenth- and nineteenth-century New England country reproductions

Shaker Workshops
1-800-840-9121
www.shakerworkshops.com
Nineteenth-century Shaker reproductions

DINING ROOM FURNITURE—MANUFACTURERS

Baker
1-800-59-baker
www.bakerfurniture.com
Eighteenth- and nineteenth-century Georgian and Federal reproductions, including the Historic Charleston collection, and contemporary styles

Broyhill
1-800-3-BROYHILL
www.broyhillfurn.com
Eighteenth- and nineteenth-century Early American, Colonial American, Shaker, and Mission adaptations, including the Attic

Heirlooms Collection, Country English, Country French, Cottage Victorian, and modern styles

Century
1-800-852-5552
www.centuryfurniture.com
Eighteenth-century Georgian and French adaptations, including the Oscar de la Renta Collection

Councill
336-859-2155
www.councill.com
Eighteenth- and nineteenth-century Georgian and Federal reproductions and adaptations

Craftique
1-919-563-1212
www.craftiquefurniture.com
Eighteenth- and nineteenth-century Colonial American and Federal reproductions including the Biltmore Estates collection

Deerfield Village
1-877-684-2156
www.deerfieldvillage.com
Eighteenth- and nineteenth-century New England country reproductions

Eldred Wheeler
1-800-779-5310
www.eldredwheeler.com
Eighteenth-century Colonial American reproductions

Ethan Allen
1-888-324-3571
www.ethanallen.com
Eighteenth- and nineteenth-century Colonial American, Shaker, Mission, French Provincial, Country French and Country Swedish adaptations, and contemporary styles

Frederick Duckloe
    1-800-882-0186
    www.duckloe.com
    Eighteenth- and nineteenth-century New England and Pennsylvania reproductions and adaptations

Fremarc
    1-800-999-0802
    www.fremarc.com
    Eighteenth-century Early English, Country English, French Provincial, and Country French reproductions and adaptations

Ficks Reed
    1-513-985-0606
    www.ficksreed.com
    Contemporary and traditional rattan and wicker

Grange
    1-800-GRANGE1
    www.grange.com
    Nineteenth-century French Country adaptations

Guy Chaddock
    661-395-5960
    www.guychaddock.com
    Eighteenth-century Early English, Country English, French Provincial, and Country French reproductions

Harden
    315-245-1000
    www.harden.com
    Eighteenth-century Colonial American reproductions

Henkel-Harris
    540-667-4900
    www.henkleharris.com
    Eighteenth-century Georgian and Federal adaptations

Henredon
> 1-800-444-3682
> www.henredon.com
> Eighteenth- and nineteenth-century Georgian, Regency, Empire, Victorian, Louis XV, and Louis XVI adaptations

Hickory Chair
> 1-800-349-4579
> www.hickorychair.com
> Eighteenth-century Georgian and Federal reproductions and adaptations, including the James River and Mount Vernon collections

Hitchcock Chairs
> 1-800-379-7932
> www.hitchcockchair.com
> Eighteenth- and nineteenth-century Early American, Colonial American, and Shaker adaptations, including the signature Lambert Hitchcock chair, Country English, and Country French

James Dew
> 1-800-272-4546
> www.jamesdew.com
> Eighteenth- and nineteenth-century Colonial American and New England country reproductions

Kincaid
> 1-800-242-1671
> www.kincaidfurniture.com
> Eighteenth- and nineteenth-century Early American, Colonial American, American Victorian, Shaker, and Mission adaptations, and modern styles

Kindel
> 616-243-3676
> www.kindelfurniture.com
> Eighteenth- and nineteenth-century Georgian and Federal reproductions, including the Wintherthur collection

Kittinger
> 716-876-1000
> www.kittingerfurniture.com
> Eighteenth- and nineteenth-century Georgian and Federal reproductions and adaptations

Knoll
> 1-800-445-5045
> www.knoll.com
> Twentieth-century Bauhaus reproductions

Lane
> 1-800-FOR-LANE
> www.lanefurniture.com
> Eighteenth- and nineteenth-century colonial and country reproductions and adaptations, including the Country Living collection

Lane Venture
> 1-800-235-3558
> www.laneventure.com
> Contemporary and traditional wicker

Lexington
> 1-800-LEX-INFO
> www.lexington.com
> Eighteenth- and nineteenth-century Early American, Colonial American, American Victorian, and Country styles, including the Bob Timberlake and Waverly collections, and modern styles

Lloyd Flanders
> 1-888-227-8252
> www.lloydflanders.com
> Contemporary and traditional wicker, including Cottage Victorian adaptations

McGuire
> 1-800-662-4847
> www.mcguirefurniture.com
> Contemporary and traditional wicker and rattan

Maine Cottage
1-207-846-1430
www.mainecottage.com
Nineteenth-century Cottage Victorian adaptations

Nichols & Stone
978-632-2770
www.nicholsandstone.com
Eighteenth- and nineteenth century Early American, Colonial American, Shaker, and Country French adaptations

Pennsylvania House
570-523-1285
www.pennsylvaniahouse.com
Eighteenth-century and nineteenth-century Colonial American, and Shaker adaptations

Pierce Martin
1-800-334-8701
www.piercemartin.com
Transitional wicker, rattan, and iron

Suter's
1-800-252-2131
www.suters.com
Eighteenth-century Colonial American reproductions

Statton
1-800-841-0225
www.statton.com
Eighteenth-century Colonial American reproductions

Stickley
315-682-5500
www.stickley.com
Eighteenth-century Colonial American reproductions and nineteenth- century Mission reissues

Thomasville
1-800-225-0265
www.thomasville.com
Eighteenth- and nineteenth-century Colonial American, Shaker, and Mission adaptations, and contemporary styles, including the Humphrey Bogart collection

Wright Table Company
828-437-2766
Eighteenth- and nineteenth-century Early American, Colonial American, Shaker, Country English, and Country French adaptations

FABRIC AND WALL COVERING

Brunschwig & Fils
1-800-538-1880
www.brunschwig&fils.com
Fabric and wallpaper including Historic Deerfield and Winterthur reproductions

Clarence House
1-800-231-0038
www.clarencehouse.com
Fabric and wallpaper

Greef
1-888-298-2991
www.greef.com
Fabric

Imperial
1-800-539-5399
www.ihdg.com
Wallpaper and fabric including Historic Charleston reproductions by Katzenbach and Warren, and Winterthur reproductions by Van Luit

Kravet
: 1-888-457-2838
www.kravet.com
Fabric and wallpaper, including the Laura Ashley Fabric Library, and Winterthur reproductions

Laura Ashley
: 1-800-367-2000
www.laura-ashleyusa.com
Fabric and wallpaper

Lee Jofa
: 1-800-455-5632
www.leejofa.com
Fabric and wallpaper

Pierre Deux
: 1-888-743-7732
www.pierredeux.com
Fabric and wallpaper in French Provincial and Country French patterns

Robert Allen
: 1-800-240-8189
Fabric and wallpaper

Scalamandre
: 1-800-932-4361
www.scalamandre.com
Fabric and wallpaper

Schumacher
: 1-800-523-1200
www.fschumacher.com
Fabric and wallpaper, including Colonial Williamsburg reproductions

Waverly
: 1-800-423-5881
www.waverly.com
Fabric and wallpaper

MILLWORK

New England Classic
1-888-460-6324
www.newenglandclassic.com
Chair rails, crown molding, and wainscoting, including Colonial American, Mission, Shaker, and Cottage Victorian

PAINT

Benjamin Moore
1-800-6PAINT6
www.benjaminmoore.com

Colonial Williamsburg Colors by Martin Senour
1-800-MSP-5270
www.martinsenour.com

Devoe
1-800-627-1650
www.devoe.com

Fuller O'Brien
www.fullerobrien.com

Glidden
1-800-627-1650
www.gliddenpaint.com

Olde Century Colors
1-800-222-3092
www.oldecenturycolors.com
Eighteenth- and nineteenth-century reproduction colors, including milk paint

Pittsburgh Paints
1-800-441-9695
www.ppgof.com

Sherwin-Williams
1-800-4SHERWIN
www.sherwin-williams.com

Winterthur at Home by H. F. Legacy
302-575-0347
www.winterthurathome.com

FLOOR COVERINGS—HARD

Armstrong
1-888-ARMSTRONG
www.armstrongfloors.com

Bruce
1-800-722-4647
www.brucelaminatefloors.com
www.brucewoodfloors.com

Mannington
1-800-FLOORUS (356-6787)
www.mannington.com

FLOOR COVERINGS—SOFT

Claire Murray
1-800-252-4733
www.clairemurray.com
Hand-hooked rugs, including Colonial Williamsburg, Historic Charleston, and Winterthur reproductions

Classic Rugs
1-888-334-0063
www.classicrug.com
Laser-cut quilt pattern rugs

Karastan
1-800-234-1120
www.karastan.com
Carpet and rugs, including Colonial Williamsburg reproductions

Pir International
1-800-621-1244
www.pirinternational.com
Oriental, French, Ethnic, contemporary and modern styles

Shaw
1-800-282-7429
www.shawrugs.com
Carpet and rugs including Winterthur reproductions

Woodard
1-800-332-7847
www.woodardweave.com
Nineteenth-century flat-woven American rugs, including Amish and Shaker reproductions

Yankee Pride
1-781-848-7610
www.yankee-pride.com
Braided, flat-woven, and hooked rugs

WINDOW TREATMENTS

Country Curtains
1-800-456-0321
www.countrycurtains.com
Wide selection of soft window treatments

Graber
1-888-554-3228
www.springs.com

Hunter Douglas
1-800-937-STYLE
www.hunterdouglas.com

Smith + Noble Windoware
1-800-248-8888
www.smithandnoble.com
Wide selection of hard and soft window treatments

LIGHTING

Baldwin Brass
1-800-566-1986
www.baldwinhardware.com
Eighteenth-century reproductions

Period Lighting
1-800-828-6990
www.periodlighting.com
Seventeenth-, eighteenth-, and nineteenth-century American reproductions

Virginia Metalcrafters
1-800-368-1002
www.vametal.com
Eighteenth-century reproductions, including Colonial Williamsburg, Historic Charleston, Mount Vernon, and Winterthur reproductions

Wildwood
1-800-733-1396
www.wildwoodlamps.com
Eighteenth-century reproductions, including Colonial Williamsburg and Mount Vernon reproductions

TABLEWARE

China

Arabia
1-800-448-8252
www.designar.com
Porcelain

Aynsley
1-800-822-1824
www.reedbarton.com
Bone china

Bennington
1-800-205-8033
www.
Stoneware and coordinating stainless, glassware, and table linens

Bernadaud
1-800-884-7775
www.bernadaud.net
Porcelain and coordinating table linens

Dedham
1-800-RABBITS (722-2487)
www.hareloom.com
Earthenware

Denby
1-800-DENBY4U (336-2948)
www.denbyusa.com
Stoneware and coordinating glassware and table linens

Fitz & Floyd
1-800-527-9550
www.fitzandfloyd.com
Bone china, porcelain, earthenware

Franciscan
1-800-955-1550
www.wedgwoodusa.com
Earthenware and coordinating stainless and glassware

Haviland
1-800-793-7106
www.haviland-limoges.com
Porcelain

Herend
1-800-643-7363
www.herendusa.com
Porcelain

Homer Laughlin
   1-800-452-4462
   www.hlchina.com
   Porcelain including Fiesta and Colonial Williamsburg reproductions

Hutschenreuther
   1-800-804-8070
   www.rosenthalchina.com
   Porcelain

Isis
   1-888-414-8448
   www.isisceramics.com
   Delftware

Johnson
   1-800-955-1550
   www.wedgwoodusa.com
   Earthenware

Lenox
   1-800-63-LENOX (635-3669)
   www.lenox.com
   Fine china and coordinating silver, stainless, and crystal

Luneville
   1-800-641-4808
   www.blachere.com
   Faience

Lynn Chase
   1-800-228-9909
   www.lynnchasedesigns.com
   Porcelain

Mariposa
   1-800-788-1304
   www.mariposa-gift.com
   Majolica

Meissen
1-866-977-9236
www.meissen.de
Porcelain

Mikasa
1-800-833-4681
www.mikasa.com
Bone china, fine china, and coordinating crystal; stoneware, and coordinating stainless and glassware

Monroe
1-800-525-4471
www.monroesaltworks.com
Stoneware

Mottahedeh
1-800-242-3050
www.mottahedeh.com
Porcelain including Colonial Williamsburg, Historic Charleston, Metropolitan Museum of Art, Monticello, and Winterthur reproductions.

Nicholas Mosse
1-877-807-3586
www.nicholasmosse.com
Earthenware

Nikko
1-201-863-5200
e-mail: custserv@nikkoceramics.com
Fine china and ironstone, including collections by folk artists Deb Moses and Charles Wysocki

Noritake
1-800-562-1991
www.noritakechina.com
China, bone china, and coordinating crystal; stoneware and coordinating glassware

Pfaltzgraff
1-800-999-2811
www.pfaltzgraff.com
Stoneware and coordinating stainless, glassware, and table linens

Pickard
1-847-395-3800
www.pickardchina.com
Fine china

Portmeirion
1-888-723-1471
www.portmeirion.com
Earthenware

Quimper
1-888-276-7799
www.quimperfaience.com
Faience and coordinating stainless

Raynaud
1-877-232-9312
www.devinecorp.net
Porcelain

Richard Ginori
1-800-215-1193
www.richardginori.1735.com
Bone china, fine china, and coordinating crystal

Robert Haviland and C. Parlon
1-800-993-2580
Porcelain

Rorstrand
1-800-448-8252
www.designor.com
Bone china, porcelain

Rosenthal
1-800-804-8070
www.rosenthalchina.com
Porcelain

Rowe
1-800-356-7687
www.rowepottery.com
Stoneware

Royal Albert
1-800-68-CHINA (682-4462)
www.royaldoultonusa.com
Bone china

Royal Copenhagen
1-800-431-1992
www.royalskandinavia.com
Porcelain

Royal Crown Derby
1-866-DERBYUS (337-2987)
www.royal-crown-derby.co.uk
Bone china

Royal Doulton
1-800-68-CHINA (682-4462)
www.royaldoulton.usa.com
Bone china, fine china

Royal Worcester
1-800-257-7189
www.royal-worcester.co.uk
Bone china, porcelain

Salmon Falls
1-800-621-2030
www.salmonfallsstoneware.com
Stoneware

Sango
> 1-800-228-8995
> www.sango.com
> Bone china, fine china, porcelain, and stoneware

Shard
> 1-888-296-0500
> e-mail: shard@kynd.net
> Stoneware, including New England thematics

Spode
> 1-800-257-7189
> www.spode.co.uk
> Bone china and fine earthenware, including Colonial Williamsburg reproductions

Vietri
> 1-800-277-5933
> www.vietri.com
> Earthenware, including majolica and coordinating stainless, glassware, and table linens

Villeroy & Boch
> 1-800-Villeroy (845-5376)
> www.villeroy-boch.com
> Bone china, fine china, faience, porcelain, semiporcelain, and coordinating stainless and glassware

Wedgwood
> 1-800-955-1550
> www.wedgwood-usa.com
> Bone china and earthenware, including Colonial Williamsburg reproductions

Replacement China

Replacements
> 1-800-737-5223
> www.replacements.com
> Discontinued patterns

Silver

Arte Italica
1-415-490-5722
Pewter

Buccellati
1-800-476-4800
www.buccellati.com
Silver

Chambly
1-800-641-4808
www.blachere.com
Silverplate, stainless

Christofle
1-877-Pavillon (728-4566)
www.christofle.com
Silver, silverplate, stainless, and coordinating porcelain, crystal, and table linens

Couzon
1-800-242-2774
Silverplate, stainless

Dansk
1-800-293-2675
www.dansk.com
Silverplate, stainless, and coordinating china

Ercuis
1-877-232-9312
email: devinecorp.net
Silver

Georg Jensen
1-800-431-1992
www.royalskandinavia.com
Silver, stainless

Gorham
    1-800-446-7426
    www.gorham1831.com
    Silver, stainless, and coordinating bone china and crystal

International
    1-888-747-0475
    www.syratech.com
    Silver, stainless

Kirk Stieff
    1-800-63-LENOX (635-3669)
    www.lenox.com
    Silver, stainless, including Colonial Williamsburg reproductions

Lunt
    1-800-242-2774
    www.luntsilversmiths.com
    Silver, stainless

Old World Pewter
    1-800-983-7030
    Stainless with pewter handles

Oneida
    1-800-877-6667
    www.oneida.com
    Silver, silverplate, stainless

Puiforcat
    1-800-993-2580
    Silver, silverplate

Reed & Barton
    1-800-822-1824
    www.reedbarton.com
    Silver, silverplate, and stainless, including Winterthur reproductions

Ricci
 1-800-544-2209
 Silver, stainless

Scof
 1-800-788-1304
 www.mariposa-gift.com
 Stainless with acrylic, bamboo, and wooden handles

Tiffany
 1-800-526-0649
 www.tiffany.com
 Silver, vermeil

Towle International
 1-888-747-0475
 www.syratech.com
 Silver, stainless

Wallace
 1-888-747-0475
 www.syratech.com
 Silver, stainless

Yamazaki
 1-800-441-3675
 www.yamazakitableware.com
 Stainless

Crystal and Glassware

Atlantis
 1-800-233-9054
 www.atlantiscrystal.com
 Crystal

Baccarat
 1-800-777-0100
 www.baccarat.fr
 Crystal

Daum
 1-866-BUY-DAUM (289-3286)
 www.daum-france
 Crystal

Durand
 1-800-257-7470
 www.jgdurand.com
 Crystal

Hoya
 1-800-462-4692
 www.hoyacrystal.com
 Crystal

Iittala
 1-800-448-8252
 www.iittala.com
 Glassware

Kosta Boda
 1-800-351-9842
 www.kostaboda.se
 Crystal

L. E. Smith
 1-800-537-6484
 www.lesmith.com
 Glassware

Lalique
 1-800-214-2738
 www.lalique.com
 Crystal

Libbey
	1-888-794-8469
	www.libbey.com
	Glassware

Luigi Bormioli
	1-215-750-9222
	www.luigibormioli.com
	Crystalline

Miller Rogaska
	1-800-822-1824
	www.reedbarton.com
	Crystal

Moser
	1-800-267-2155
	www.moser-glass.com
	Glassware

Orrefors
	1-800-351-9842
	www.orrefors.se
	Crystal

Saint-Louis
	1-800-238-5522
	Crystal

Salviati
	1-212-725-4361
	www.salviati.com
	Glassware

Simon Pearce
	1-800-774-5277
	www.simonpearce.com
	Glassware

Spiegelau
1-800-999-6347
www.wmf-usa.com
Glassware

Steuben
1-800-424-4240
www.steuben.com
Crystal

Varga
1-877-232-9312
e-mail: devinecorp.net
Crystal

Venini
1-866-696-9640
www.venini.it
Glassware

Waterford
1-800-955-1550
www.waterford-usa.com
Crystal and coordinating dinnerware and flatware

William Yeoward
1-800-818-8484
www.williamyeowardcrystal.com
Crystal

LINENS

Anichini
1-800-553-5309
www.anichini.com

Braun
1-800-372-7286
www.braunco.com

Frette
1-212-988-5221
www.frette.com

Leron
1-800-954-6369
www.leron.com

Porthault
1-212-688-1660
www.dporthault.com

Pratesi
1-800-332-6925
www.eluxury.com

Schweitzer
1-800-554-6367
www.schweitzerlinen.com

Yves Delorme
1-800-322-3911
www.yvesdelorme.com

TABLE ACCESSORIES

Gardener's Eden
1-800-822-9600
www.gardenerseden.com
Birdhouses and nests, garden animals, watering cans

Hedges
1-800-698-5656
www.designhedges.com
Boxwood, fruit, and vegetable topiaries

Lilac Rose
1-800-530-1231
www.lilacrose.com
Dried and pressed flowers, preserved greenery

Nature's Creations
1-800-450-0588
www.peopleworking.com
Fruit and vegetable candles

Petals
1-800-431-2464
www.petals.com
Silk floral arrangements

Viking Woodcrafts, Inc.
1-800-328-0116
www.vikingwoodcrafts.com
Unfinished wooden place mats, plates, and napkin rings

Chocolates

Green Mountain
1-800-886-1249
www.greenmountainchocolate.com

Godiva
1-800-9-GODIVA
www.godiva.com

Lake Champlain
1-800-634-8105
www.lakechamplainchocolates.com

Storage

Eureka
1-800-376-8209
www.woodchest.com
Silver keepers

Hagerty
1-800-348-5162
www.hagerty-polish.com
Silver keepers

Table Pads

    Sentry
        1-800-328-7237

MAIL ORDER CATALOGS

    Albert Smyth
        1-800-638-3333
        www.albertsmyth.com
        Tableware

    Ballard
        1-800-367-2775
        www.ballarddesigns.com
        Home furnishings and accessories

    Bombay Company
        1-800-829-7789
        www.bombayco.com
        Home furnishings and accessories

    Crate & Barrel
        1-800-967-6696
        www.crateandbarrel.com
        Home furnishings, tableware, and accessories

    Gracious Style
        1-888-828-7170
        www.graciousstyle.com
        Table linens

    Michael C. Fina
        1-800-389-3462
        www.michaelcfina.com
        Tableware

    Pottery Barn
        1-800-922-9934
        www.potterybarn.com
        Home furnishings, tableware, and accessories

Ross-Simons
1-800-556-7376
www.ross-simons.com
Tableware

Williams-Sonoma
1-800-541-1262
www.williams-sonoma.com
Linens and tableware

Your Style at a Glance

See pages 124 and 125 for a chart that combines all of the elements of decorating your dining area to match your style. On pages 126 and 127 you will find a blank chart that you can fill in with your own ideas for decorating your dining area and filling it with your own china, silver, crystal, and table linens.

STYLE	FURNITURE	FABRICS	WALL COVERINGS	FLOOR COVERINGS
Formal	Queen Anne Georgian, including Chippendale, Hepplewhite, and Sheraton Regency Federal, including Hepplewhite, Sheraton, Duncan Phyfe Louis XV Louis XVI Gustavian Victorian Contemporary	Silk, satin; textures such as brocade, brocatelle, damask, moiré, shantung, and strié; taffeta; velvet; leather	Ceiling medallions and detailed crown molding, chair rails, mirror panels, period paneling, specific paint, specific wall covering	Glazed ceramic tile; polished stone such as granite, marble, or slate; polished wood in parquet or strip; sculptured carpet; velvet carpet; French rugs; Oriental rugs
Semi-formal	Early English, Colonial American, including Queen Anne, Chippendale French Provincial Italian Provincial Swedish Provincial American Victorian	Cotton; linen including crewel work; wool; textures such as matalasse and tapestry; velvet; leather	Chair rails and simple crown molding; period paneling; specific paint; specific wall covering	Unglazed ceramic tile; unpolished stone such as flagstone or slate; unpolished wood in strip or random widths; textured carpet; hooked rugs; needlepoint rugs; Oriental rugs
Informal	Country English Early American Country French Country Italian Country Swedish Cottage Victorian Farmhouse Victorian Southwest, including Adobe, Mission, Santa Fe American Country, including Shaker, Pennsylvania Dutch Modern, including Bauhaus, Japanese, Scandinavian Tropical Beach	Cotton, including canvas, duck, denim, sailcloth; burlap; corduroy; flannel; hopsacking; tweed; twill; union cloth; woven textures	Chair rails and simple crown molding; open beams and rafters; period paneling; specific paint; specific wall covering	Brick; Mexican or terra-cotta tile; unpolished stone such as flagstone or slate; unpolished wood in strip or random widths with or without pegs; stenciled wood; textured carpet; braided rugs; rag rugs; ethnic rugs, sisal matting; painted floorcloths

WINDOW TREATMENTS	ACCESSORIES	CHINA	SILVER	CRYSTAL	TABLE LINENS
Curtains such as straight panels or tie-backs, used alone or with a cornice, swag and jabot, or valance; Austrian shades; Venetian blinds; vertical blinds	Crystal, marble, porcelain, silver, leather, wood	China, porcelain	Silver, vermeil	Clear crystal, plain or gold or platinum rims; clear crystal, cut, cased, engraved, or etched; colored crystal; iridescent crystal	Formal textures, such as damask, moiré and strié; lace, including appliqué and cutwork; organdy, appliquéd or embroidered
Curtains such as straight panels or tie-backs, used alone or with a cornice, swag and jabot, or valance; fabric shades such as Roman, balloon, pleated, or plain; shutters, painted or stained; shutters with fabric inserts; blinds such as mini-blinds, Venetian, or vertical	Brass, pewter, ceramics, leather, wood	China, porcelain	Silver, silver plate, stainless steel, stainless steel with contrasting handles such as porcelain or pewter	Clear crystal, plain or simply cut colored crystal, semi-opaque	Cotton and linen prints, such as florals, including botanicals, chinoiserie, and Jacobean; toiles, either floral or scenic; plaids and stripes; cotton and linen solids
Curtains such as straight panels or tie-backs with a simple valance, café and tab curtains; mini or woven wood blinds; shutters, painted or stained; roller fabric shades; shoji screens	Copper, pottery, tin, wrought iron, leather, wood	China, porcelain, earthernware, woodenware	Silver, silver plate, stainless steel, stainless steel with contrasting handles such as bamboo, bone, horn, Lucite, plastic pewter, and wood	Clear crystal, plain, uncut and undecorated; colored crystal, opaque; milk glass	Cotton prints including small-scale florals and fruits; paisleys and paisley stripes; checks, plaids, and stripes, thematics; cotton solids including burlap, denim, duck, and woven textures

Your Style at a Glance Worksheet

STYLE	FURNITURE	FABRICS	WALL COVERINGS	FLOOR COVERINGS

WINDOW TREATMENTS	ACCESSORIES	CHINA	SILVER	CRYSTAL	TABLE LINENS

INDEX

Amelung, John Frederick, 63
American Country style, 14, 29, 50
American Provincial style, 14
American Victorian style, 14, 24, 98, 99
Anichini, 72, 119
anniversaries, 92
antiques, 31
appliqué, 71
Arabia, 40, 107

Baccarat, 62, 116
barware, 67
Bauhaus, 99
beach furniture, 14, 30
Bernadaud, 39, 107
birthdays, 92
Bottger, Johann Fredrich, 39
Braun, 72, 119
buffet table setting, 79–80, 86

candles, 91, 120
catalogs, 121–22
china, 35–46, 60, 66, 70, 81, 88; caring for, 45; choosing pattern, 37–40; replacements, 113; shopping for, 41–45; storing, 46; vendors of, 107–13
china, bone, 37, 39, 88–89, 107–8, 111–13, 114

china, fine, 37, 45–46
Chippendale style, 13, 17, 50
Christmas decorations, 92–93
Colonial American style, 13, 22, 95–101, 103
contemporary style, 13, 15, 21, 97, 101
costs, estimating, 8–10
Cottage Victorian style, 14, 27, 96, 100, 103
cotton, 70–71, 76
Country English style, 14, 15, 25, 96, 97, 98, 101
Country French style, 14, 15, 26, 96, 97, 98, 100, 101
Country Italian style, 14, 26
Country Swedish style, 14, 26, 97
Country Victorian style, 14
creamware, 37–38
crystal, 59–68, 81, 109, 110, 111; caring for, 67–68; choosing, 60–63; shopping for, 63–67; storing, 68; vendors of, 116–19
crystal, lead, 60
crystal, full lead, 60
crystalline, 60
cutwork, 71

damask, 71
decorations, 87–88, 91–92, 121
dining area planning chart, 11–12

dining chairs, 32
dining room furniture, 95–96
dining tables, 32

earthenware, 37–38, 40, 46, 70, 89, 107–8, 110, 112–13
eclectic style, 5
Early American style, 14, 15, 25, 35, 95, 98, 99, 100, 101
Early English style, 13, 22, 97
Easter decorations, 93
embroidery, 71
engagements, 92

fabrics, 101–3
fabric patterns, 71, 76
family occasions, 92
Farmhouse Victorian style, 14, 28
Father's Day decorations, 94
Federal style, 13, 20, 95, 96, 98, 99
floor covering, 8, 104–5
floral arrangements, 89–90, 120
formal dinner setting, 78, 81–83
formal style, 4, 13, 16–21, 36, 47, 59, 69, 90
Franciscan, 40
French Provincial style, 13, 23, 50, 97
Frette, 71, 119
furniture adaption, 31, 95–101
furniture collection, 31
furniture group, 31
furniture suite, 31

Georgian style, 13, 15, 16, 95, 96, 98, 99
Ginori, Richard, 39–40
glass, 60
glass, blown, 60–61
glass, cased, 62

glass, colored, 61
glass, frosted, 62
glass, milk, 61
glass, pressed, 60–61
glass, wine, 64–66
glassware, 116–19
gold plate, 49, 56
Gracious Style, 72, 122
graduations, 92
Gustavian style, 13, 20

Halloween, 94
Haviland, 39
hemstitch, 71
Hepplewhite style, 13, 17
holidays, 92–94
hollowware, 55
home equity loan, 10
Homer Laughlin, 40

informal style, 5, 14, 25–30, 36, 47, 59, 69, 74, 90
ironstone, 38, 110
Italian Provincial style, 14, 23

Jarves, Deming, 63

Kennedy, Jackie, 49
Kosta Boda, 62, 117

L. E. Smith, 62, 117
lace, 71
Lalique, 62, 117
Lenox, 40, 109
Lenox, Walter Scott, 40
Leron, 72, 119
Libbey, William L., 63
lighting, 8, 106
linens, 70, 76, 119–20

Louis XV style, 13, 15, 19, 35, 98
Louis XVI style, 13, 15, 20, 98
luncheon table setting, 79, 84
lustreware, 61

millwork, 103
Mission style, 13, 97, 98, 101, 103
modern style, 14, 29, 35, 96, 98, 99, 101
monograms, 55, 75, 76
Mother's Day decorations, 93–94

napkins, 74–75, 76, 78
New England Glass Company, 63
New Year's Eve decorations, 93
Noritaki, 40

opaline, 61
Orrefors, 62, 117

paint, 103–4
pewter, 49–50, 56, 113, 115
Pfaltzgraff, 40, 110
place mats, 73, 76, 77
place settings, 41–43, 51–53, 64, 81–86
porcelain, 37, 39–40, 60, 70, 88, 107–13
Porthault, 71, 119
potted plants, 90
Pratesi, 71, 119

Queene Anne style, 13, 15, 16

rayon, 76
Regency style, 13, 18, 98
reproduction, 31, 95–101
Rorstrand, 40, 111
Royal Copenhagen, 40, 111

semi-formal dinner setting, 79, 83–84
semi-formal style, 4–5, 13–14, 22–24, 36, 47, 59, 69, 90
Saint-Louis, 62, 118
Schweitzer, 72, 120
semiporcelain, 37
serveware, 67
serving pieces, 32, 43–44, 53–54
Shaker style, 13, 95, 97, 98, 100, 101, 103
Sheraton style, 13, 18
silver, 47–57, 60, 66, 81, 109; caring for, 56; choosing pattern, 48–50; shopping for, 50–55; storing, 56–57; vendors of, 113–16
silver plate, 49, 56, 113–16
silver, sterling, 48–49, 56
Southwest style, 14, 28
Spiegelau, 62
Spode, Josiah, 39
stainless steel, 50, 56, 109, 110, 113–16
Stiegel, "Baron," 63
stoneware, 38, 40, 46, 107, 109, 110–12
Swedish Provincial style, 14, 24

table: accessories, 91, 120–22; decorating a, 87–94; dressing a, 77–80; setting a, 81–86
table linens, 69–76, 77–78, 107, 110, 113, 122; caring for, 76; choosing, 70–72; monograms on, 75; shopping for, 72–75; storing, 76
table runners, 74, 76, 77
tablecloths, 72–73, 76, 77

tableware, vendors of, 107–113, 121–22
Thanksgiving decorations, 94
Tropical style, 14, 30

Valentine's Day decorations, 92–93
vermeil, 49, 56, 115
Victorian style, 13, 14, 21, 98

wall coverings, 8–9, 101–3
Waterford, 62, 119
Wedgwood, 39, 113
White House, 40
window treatments, 9–10, 105–6
Wistar, Casper, 63
wood, types of, 31

NOTES